ENCOUNTERING THE SUPERNATURAL

Discover God's amazing
presence and power for your life

Books in This Series

When God Seems Silent

Battle Cry for Your Marriage

Finding Freedom

Straight Talk To Leaders

Encountering the Supernatural

The TIME Is NOW! Series

ENCOUNTERING THE SUPERNATURAL

Discover God's amazing
presence and power for your life

Larry Kreider

Kevin Kazemi

Merle Shenk

House To House Publications
Lititz, Pennsylvania USA
www.h2hp.com

Encountering the Supernatural
Discover God's amazing presence and power for your life

by Larry Kreider, Kevin Kazemi and Merle Shenk

Copyright © 2018 Larry Kreider, Kevin Kazemi and Merle Shenk

Published by
House to House Publications
11 Toll Gate Road, Lititz, PA 17543 USA
Telephone: 800.848.5892
www.h2hp.com

ISBN-10: 0-9987574-4-6
ISBN-13: 978-0-9987574-4-5

Unless otherwise noted, all scripture quotations in this publication are taken from the *Holy Bible, New International Version* (NIV).
© 1973, 1978, 1984 by International Bible Society. Used by permission of Zondervan Publishing House. All rights reserved.

All rights reserved. No portion of this book may be reproduced without the permission of the publisher.

CONTENTS

How to Use This Resource 6
Introduction 9

1. **Exploring the Supernatural**
   Larry Kreider 11
2. **Experiencing the Fear of the Lord**
   Kevin Kazemi 31
3. **A Visitation from God**
   Kevin Kazemi 51
4. **Being Changed by His Presence**
   Kevin Kazemi 69
5. **Experiencing His Presence**
   Merle Shenk 89
6. **Ministering with Jesus**
   Merle Shenk 113
7. **Growing in a Supernatural Lifestyle**
   Merle Shenk 135
8. **You Too can Encounter the Supernatural!**
   Larry Kreider 157

Endnotes 181
Teaching Outlines 184
Journaling space for reflection questions 200
Steps to being filled with the Holy Spirit 217

How to Use This Resource

Personal study
Read from start to finish and receive personal revelation. Learn spiritual truths to help yourself and others.
- Each reading includes questions for personal reflection and space for journaling at the end of the book.

Daily devotional
Eight weeks of daily readings with corresponding questions for personal reflection and journaling.
- Each chapter is divided into seven sections for weekly use.
- Each day includes reflection questions and space to journal.

Mentoring relationship
When this book is used as a one-on-one discipling/mentoring tool, questions can be answered and life applications discussed.

- A spiritual mentor can easily take a person they are mentoring through these short Bible study lessons and use the reflection questions for dialogue about what is learned.
- Study each day's entry or an entire chapter at a time.

Small group study
Study in a small group setting or in a class or Bible study group.

- The teacher uses the material in the outline provided at the end of the book. Everyone in the group reads the chapter and discusses the questions together.

Acknowledgments

As authors, we are grateful to a number of people who made this project possible: Diane Omondi and Lou Ann Good for their skillful editing; Peter Bunton for reading the manuscript cover to cover and offering valuable insights; Nancy Leatherman and Natalie Teufel for their indispensable expertise as proofreaders; and Sarah Sauder and House to House Publications for making this book become a reality.

Our heartfelt thanks goes to numerous leaders in the body of Christ and in the DOVE International family who taught us countless spiritual insights that helped to shape this book.

Most of all, we give thanks to the God of our Lord Jesus Christ who desires for each of us to experience His supernatural power and presence.

— Larry Kreider, Kevin Kazemi and Merle Shenk

Encountering the Supernatural

Introduction

Encountering a supernatural God in everyday life is not only for a chosen few. It is for everyone, including you.

Do you desire to connect with God supernaturally, but feel helpless, confused, or uncertain? The purpose of this book is to awaken you to the reality that Jesus wants you to experience His presence and that He wants to perform supernatural works through you. He wants to open your eyes to the reality of the spiritual realm.

I (Larry) am honored to co-author this book with Kevin Kazemi and Merle Shenk. As authors, we draw from a wide range of experiences from different parts of the world. Kevin was born into a Muslim family in Iran. When he was a young man, God met him supernaturally. He shares in this book about the encounters he had with the Lord and how these have shaped his life and ministry. Merle and his wife Cheree spent more than eleven years as missionaries in South Africa where they experienced the supernatural power of God again and again. Merle has written about many of the times when God's supernatural power has worked through him, and what we need to do as God's children to walk in that power. I am privileged to witness God working supernaturally and to hear first-hand stories of the supernatural power of God in many nations, including our own nation of America. Many of these stories are shared in the pages of this book.

Each of us as authors had our own revelation from God regarding how we encountered the Lord supernaturally in everyday life. And we are still learning how to live a supernatural life that gives glory to God.

Paul the apostle said, "He (Jesus) did not come in wisdom of men. . . but in the demonstration of the spirit and power so our faith does not rest on the wisdom of men but on the power of God" (I Corinthians 2:4).

This is our prayer for you as you join us on this journey of encountering the supernatural. The Lord desires for you to experience His power and His presence as He works supernaturally through you day by day.

Larry Kreider, Kevin Kazemi and Merle Shenk

CHAPTER 1

Exploring the Supernatural

Larry Kreider

DAY 1

The Supernatural World We Live In

A few years ago, I was riding to the Dallas Fort Worth airport after a Sunday worship service in a huge pick-up truck owned by a Texan businessman (everything in Texas is big!). He was telling me that he and his wife were childless for many years, and it was a great struggle for them. They tried everything they could, and the doctors gave them no hope of having a child. As he drove into the airline terminal, a supernatural gift of faith rose up in my heart for this couple to conceive a child. As I opened the door and stepped out of his truck, I reached across the seat and grabbed his hand. I spoke into his life that he and his wife would be conceiving a child in the near future.

At first it kind of frightened me to hear myself speaking those words. I did not want to give them false hope, but I felt strongly that the Lord had given me a supernatural message for this young Texan.

A year later, when I was back in the same church, the businessman and his wife walked up to me before the service began. They showed me their new baby boy who was conceived within a month of my foretelling that he and his wife would conceive a child. The businessman told me that when I spoke those words to him in his pickup truck, he felt a surge go through his body and he knew that the Lord had done something supernatural.

Let's get the facts straight. If God can use me, He can use anybody! Our God wants to teach each one of us to encounter Him in our everyday lives so He can work through us supernaturally to touch and transform the lives of those around us.

Let's talk about the supernatural world we live in. The supernatural world around us is as real as the chair in which you sit, the car that you drive, and the food that you eat. Although the supernatural world often cannot be detected by the human eye, I assure you, it is more influential in our lives than the things we can taste, see and feel. God desires to open our eyes so that we can perceive the unseen realm and discover the spiritual reasons for things that happen in our natural world.

The forces within the supernatural include God, angels, Satan, and demons. The supernatural powers of God and Satan are certainly not equal in power but they are both in competition for the destiny of our lives. We can tap into either source—and experience either havoc or abundant life (John 10:10).

> God desires to open our eyes to perceive the unseen realm and discover the spiritual reasons for things that happen in our natural world.

I remember watching a puppet show when I was a child. At first, I thought the puppets were talking and moving on their own. Eventually I realized that something was happening behind the scenes that I could not see. Someone was manipulating the puppets and making them move. By themselves, the puppets could not talk, walk or move at all.

As humans, we are not mindless puppets with someone pulling our strings forcing us to act according to their whims. But we often are manipulated by the supernatural world and made to do, say and believe things we would never do, say or believe on our own. God through His Holy Spirit creates the desire within us to live wholeheartedly for Him. He wants to unleash His power in our lives to experience the supernatural realm that takes authority over every act of the devil. Satan and his demons are determined to drown out the voice of the Holy Spirit by inserting lies, unbelief and questions that are meant to destroy God's work. Both the good and bad forces of the supernatural influence us. That is why God desires to open our spiritual eyes.

REFLECTION
Is what we perceive always accurate? Explain why or why not.

We tend to focus on what we can see with our natural eyes rather than seeking spiritual insight. This was true even in Old Testament times. In 2 Kings 6, Elisha's servant was terrified because an enemy king had surrounded the city with his army. Distraught by what he understood as impending doom, the servant wrung his hands and whimpered, "What shall we do? What shall we do?" Elisha calmly replied, "There are more with us than with them" (2 Kings 6:16). This viewpoint made absolutely no sense to the servant until God opened his eyes to the supernatural spirit world. Suddenly the servant saw the reality of what was happening in the spirit realm around him. The hills were actually filled with angels who vastly outnumbered the army of the enemy king. This spiritual insight changed his perspective on everything.

Experiences like these are not relegated to the times when the Bible was written. The Spirit of God is still at work today! God is still revealing the supernatural to us in our generation.

People throughout the world today often feel helpless due to the situations they find themselves in. They cry out with frenzied begging. Too often they think God doesn't hear their cries because they do not see Him at work. But God does not want us to fear or shrivel in defeat. God does not want us to behave like mindless puppets, tossed about by unseen forces. Instead, God wants to teach us to experience His supernatural power and presence in our daily lives in the midst of whatever circumstances we might be experiencing.

Like Elisha, pray that your eyes will be opened so that you will see from God's perspective the unseen world of God's power and experience His presence all around us. "His divine power has given us everything we need for a godly life through our knowledge of him who called us by his own glory and goodness" (2 Peter 1:3).

Being Born Again is a Supernatural Experience

Those of us who serve Christ each have our own "God story"; the account of how we gave our lives to Christ and the difference the Lord has made in our lives. Paul the Apostle gave his God story to King Agrippa, which is recorded in Acts 26. Paul told about his life before conversion, the circumstances surrounding his conversion, and the change in his life after he was converted to follow Christ on the road to Damascus. The supernatural events leading to Paul's conversion thrill us.

When we tell our own stories, we often emphasize our own role in making a decision to follow Christ. But what is more amazing is that the God of the universe invaded our lives. God is the one who has drawn us to Himself (John 6:44). That process and event is supernatural. The Scriptures tell us the angels in heaven rejoice when one sinner repents (Luke 15:10). Our decision to receive Christ releases something supernatural in the heavens!

> A true conversion is a supernatural experience!

Jesus told Nicodemus that he must be born again in order to experience the kingdom of God (John 3:3). At first, Nicodemus could not understand this concept. He contemplated whether he would need to go back into his mother's womb. But Jesus taught Nicodemus that he would need to be born again spiritually to become a brand-new person! It was a supernatural experience!

My story of giving my life completely to Christ at age eighteen started with God convicting me of my sin of being backslidden. I had received Christ into my life when

I was eleven years of age, but I had not grown spiritually during the next seven years and my spiritual heart became cold towards the Lord. When I surrendered completely to Christ at eighteen, I was literally transformed. I thought differently. I looked different. The next day, my girlfriend knew immediately that I was changed. The Scriptures call this becoming a new creation in Christ (2 Corinthians 5:17). It is a supernatural work of God!

I meet so many believers who sell themselves short by not recognizing the supernatural power of God in their lives when they are born again. We need to have the expectation that we will be different and begin living a supernatural life. The Scriptures teach us that Christ lives in us! "I have been crucified with Christ and I no longer live, but Christ lives in me" (Galatians 2:20).

REFLECTION

How are you experiencing the supernatural life of Christ in your life today?

A true conversion is a supernatural experience! Salvation is not merely mental assent to a truth in the Bible. Too many people are trying to live like Jesus by copying His life and living by His principles rather than submitting totally to Him and experiencing a supernatural life!

We need to have a mindset change. Take a moment and fathom this truth: Christ, the God above all gods, lives in us. Christ living within us is the starting place for a life of supernatural power. Let's reach out to the Lord today, and receive His grace to live the supernatural life that He has called each of us to live. He is patiently waiting for you to live by faith and experience His supernatural power and presence.

DAY 3: Holy Spirit Baptism Releases the Supernatural

Being baptized in the Holy Spirit takes us to a new level of power and opens us up to God's supernatural world. It changes how we see things. It increases our faith. It is a bit like putting on glasses and seeing things we never saw before.

I served for fifteen years as a local pastor and for many years saw people baptized in the Holy Spirit almost every Sunday. Baptism in the Holy Spirit changed them forever. Healing became possible. Freedom from addictions became possible. They now believed God could do anything for them if they believed by faith. God was not just up in heaven, but He was on the earth changing lives and doing miracles by His Holy Spirit for all who would believe Him.

All genuine believers have the Spirit of God dwelling in them. First Corinthians 3:16 says, "Don't you know that you yourselves are God's temple and that God's Spirit lives in you?"

When you were convicted of your sin before you received Christ, the Holy Spirit was outside of you bringing conviction. When you received Jesus, the Holy Spirit came to live within you. But there's more! The New Testament depicts two distinct yet complementary aspects of receiving the Holy Spirit. Let's compare the two experiences.

The disciples' first encounter with the Holy Spirit was when Jesus breathed on them and told them to "receive the Holy Spirit." He made it clear that their experience was still incomplete (see John 20:22). In His final words to them before His ascension, He commanded them not to go out and preach immediately, but to go back to Jerusalem and wait there until they were baptized in the Holy Spirit and thus given the power they needed to be effective witnesses. "Do not leave Jerusalem until the Father sends you the gift he promised, as I told you before. John baptized with water, but in just a few days you will be baptized with the Holy Spirit.... But you will receive power when the Holy Spirit comes upon you. And you will be my witnesses, telling people about me everywhere—in Jerusalem, throughout Judea, in Samaria, and to the ends of the earth" (Acts 1:4-5,8).

> Being filled with the Holy Spirit is the Lord's provision for releasing His power into the believer's life.

So the disciples prayed and waited. During the festival of Pentecost, 120 of His disciples were gathered together in one place, and the baptism in the Holy Spirit that Jesus told them to wait for, happened! "On the day of Pentecost all the believers were meeting together in one place. Suddenly, there was a sound from heaven… and everyone present was filled with the Holy Spirit and began speaking in other languages, as the Holy Spirit gave them this ability" (see Acts 2:1-4).

They had received the Holy Spirit only a few weeks before when Jesus breathed on them (John 20:22), but this time they were filled with the Holy Spirit. They received a new dimension of the Holy Spirit's power.

This distinction between receiving the Holy Spirit at your spiritual rebirth and being filled with the Holy Spirit is significant. Being filled with the Holy Spirit is the Lord's provision for releasing His power into the believer's life.

REFLECTION
How does being baptized in the Holy Spirit open us to the supernatural power of Jesus Christ?

Saul was on his way to Damascus to persecute the early Christians when the Lord met him. "'Who are you, Lord?' Saul asked. And the voice replied, 'I am Jesus, the one you are persecuting! Now get up and go into the city, and you will be told what you must do.' ... So Ananias went and found Saul. He laid his hands on him and said, 'Brother Saul, the Lord Jesus, who appeared to you on the road, has sent me so that you might regain your sight and be filled with the Holy Spirit'" (Acts 9:5-6,17).

Saul, who became Paul the apostle, was baptized in the Holy Spirit three days after he received Christ into his life on the Damascus road. It happened when Ananias laid his hands on Saul and prayed.

When I was baptized in the Holy Spirit in my early 20s, it opened me up to the supernatural world. I suddenly had faith to pray for people to be healed and delivered. I was changed forever!

Let's be sure we are filled and baptized with the Holy Spirit so we can experience the supernatural in new ways in our lives. We can be filled with the Holy Spirit again and again. The same disciples who were filled with the Holy Spirit in Acts 2 were again filled in Acts 4:31. Let's ask the Lord to fill us to overflowing with His power and His presence!

DAY 4 **Faith Releases the Supernatural**

Faith releases the supernatural in our lives. Jesus constantly told His disciples that they needed to have faith to experience the supernatural. He called them "you of little faith" when they were frightened in the boat when the seas became stormy (Matthew 8:26). He told them that if they had faith as small as a grain of mustard seed, they could speak to a mountain and it would be removed (Matthew 17:20). And the Bible teaches us that without faith, it is impossible to please God (Hebrews 11:6).

> God wants us to experience His supernatural life flowing through us as we believe in faith!

I have a pastor friend who grew up as a farm boy in the Dakotas. One day he accidentally left the gate in the pasture open and the 150 cows in their herd walked through the open gate and were outside the boundaries of the pasture. When he realized what had happened and knew there was no one to help him, he knew he needed a miracle. There was only one small open gate in the fence that ran for miles. He decided to speak to the cows with faith in Jesus' name to "line up in front of the gate and go through the gate back into the pasture." Those 150 cows actually lined up and walked through the one small gate opening in the long fence and back into the pasture. Amazing! This young farm boy took a step of faith and the Lord honored him with a supernatural miracle!

My wife LaVerne has a dear friend who was informed that her friend was diagnosed with leukemia. Her husband joined her to pray for this man in faith, believing the supernatural God who brings healing is more real than the natural report from a doctor. A few days later, the man was completely healed. The doctors monitoring his case were dumbfounded. The leukemia was totally gone! These friends believed God's Word in faith, and the God of the supernatural performed a modern-day miracle. "He has come to heal all of our sicknesses and all of our diseases" (Psalm 103:3).

> **REFLECTION**
> *Give an example of a time you experienced the supernatural power of God in your life.*

Exploring the Supernatural

While in Malaysia this week, I was asked a question that I am asked in many places: "What about those we pray for in faith but are not healed?" My answer is, "I would rather pray for ten persons and have only one healed, than pray for no one in faith and no one gets healed."

There are aspects about the supernatural that we do not understand fully, but we do know our God heals. He wants us to experience His supernatural life flowing through us as we believe in faith! We are not the healers, our God is. It is our responsibility to pray in faith. He has the power to heal!

DAY 5 Building Our Faith

I cannot emphasize enough the importance of reading and meditating on the Word of God to build your faith. All scripture is inspired by God (2 Timothy 3:16); reading and meditating on the Word of God builds our faith.

We must have faith to experience the supernatural in our lives. Faith comes by hearing and hearing by the Word of God (Romans 10:17). Reading the Word of God builds faith into our lives and causes us to live in the supernatural realm. Otherwise, the natural world around us blocks us from seeing God's power.

Read and listen to stories of those who have experienced the supernatural power of God in their lives. Their experiences will encourage you and take you to new levels of faith where you can experience more of the supernatural in your life. I have learned so much about faith from those I meet around the world who have learned to live by faith, believing that the Word of God is alive and powerful just like it says it is (Hebrews 4:12).

> In the New Testament, the supernatural was normal.

A few years ago, I spent a week ministering in Indonesia where I needed to speak through a translator. The Indonesian pastor who translated for me was amazing! I loved ministering alongside this pastor who had mastered the English language so perfectly.

I asked him how he had learned to speak English so well. His answer astounded me. He had grown up in a Buddhist home. One day he had a supernatural visitation from Jesus that changed his life forever. Sometime after his conversion, this man heard about an American minister who was coming to his town. With excitement he attended the meeting, but upon arrival, he was told that they were not able to find a translator. The Indonesian pastor recalled, "I found that I could understand every word the American minister was saying! So I took courage and translated for the preacher." The God of heaven gave this Indonesian the supernatural ability to understand and speak the English language. Since then, more than twenty years later, this Indonesian man continues translating for English-speaking ministers.

Exploring the Supernatural

In the New Testament, the supernatural was normal. It was the natural course of life. Jesus turned water into wine, healed people nearly everywhere He went, and raised the dead. However, in His home town, Jesus could not do many miracles due to the lack of faith in His own family and in His community (Mark 6:5-6). Faith and the supernatural go hand in hand.

Philip was translated from one place to another according to Acts 8:39-40. After Philip baptized the Ethiopian leader who had charge of all the treasury of Candace the queen of the Ethiopians, he ended up in another city without needing to take any natural transportation. No car, no bus, no horse, no airplane…he was supernaturally transported from one location to another and found himself at Azotus!

REFLECTION
Name some ways that we can practically build our faith.

I look forward to experiencing this supernatural transportation in the future. I am writing this chapter from an airport in Singapore with about forty hours of travel ahead of me before I arrive home. Being translated from one place to another supernaturally would be wonderful! That would save lots of airline expenses and many hours of travel. I recently logged more than two million miles traveling on United Airlines, so being translated like Philip would be amazing!

Supernatural provision

DAY 6

Our God is a supernatural God who desires to meet us in a miraculous way in every area of our lives. This includes supernatural provision.

We see amazing stories of supernatural provision in the Scriptures. In the days of Moses, quail and manna fell to the ground to feed the Israelites during their time of living in the wilderness. Jesus fed the five thousand with only a few fish and some small loaves of bread that multiplied when He gave thanks to His Father in heaven. When taxes needed to be paid, Jesus instructed Peter to catch a fish and use the money in the fish's mouth to pay for taxes. The same God can provide for us supernaturally today.

> A key to experiencing the supernatural is maintaining an attitude of thanksgiving.

Recently a husband and wife told me that they were trusting God for the money to send their child to university. They knew they needed a supernatural miracle. They received a small gift that could have helped with the tuition expenses, but they felt led of the Lord to give it all away to missions. Later the same day, someone handed them an envelope containing thousands of dollars that paid much of the tuition for their child's first year of university. They saw it for what it was—a supernatural miracle.

Several years ago, my family had a financial need. We were living on a very small budget and obeying God in every way that we knew how. I was praying for the Lord to provide for us financially. One morning I opened the door of our home so that I could go to work, and I saw the most amazing phenomenon. Money was lying all over the place! It was on the front lawn, the porch, and all around the house—even on the back lawn! You may ask, "How did it get there?" I have no idea. Did it ever happen again? No, but I will never forget it. All I know is that God did it, and it was a blessing to us. God is a miraculous God who answers prayers in a supernatural way.

A key to experiencing the supernatural is maintaining an attitude of thanksgiving. "In all things give thanks, for this is the will of God in Christ Jesus concerning you" (1 Thessalonians 5:18). God instructs us to refuse anxiety as we walk with Him in a constant attitude of thanksgiving. Philippians 4:6 tells us that we should "not be anxious about anything, but in everything, by prayer and petition, with thanksgiving, present your requests to God." No matter how dire the circumstances, we always have something for which to thank God.

REFLECTION
Give examples of supernatural provision from the Scriptures. Give any examples of supernatural provision that you have experienced.

For many years I have used *Matthew Henry's Concise Commentary of the Whole Bible* as a study resource. The story is told that one day a man stole Matthew Henry's wallet. At the end of the day he wrote in his diary, "First," he said, "I am thankful I have never been robbed before. Second, I am thankful he took my money and not my life. Third, I am thankful he did not take more; he could have taken my horse and my clothes as well. Next, I am thankful that what I had stolen from me really did not amount to very much. Then I am grateful that what I lost, in time, could be replaced. But, finally, and most importantly, I am thankful that I was the one robbed and not the robber!"[1] Matthew Henry had learned the secret of giving thanks in every situation.

Moses saw supernatural provision for food when God rained manna on the ground, but the next generation under Joshua experienced the Lord's supernatural provision through sowing and reaping crops. For a seed to become a fruit-bearing tree is also a supernatural phenomenon. As mentioned before, Jesus fed the five thousand supernaturally, but Jesus and His disciples' physical needs were also met by a company of people who traveled with Him and provided for Him (Luke 8:1-3). Both methods of provision were from the hand of the Lord. Both in their own way were supernatural.

Let's learn to live expectantly. God desires to use you in a supernatural way and provide for you in ways that are beyond your comprehension!

Exploring the Supernatural

Supernatural Healing

One important area of experiencing the supernatural is that of healing. Mark 16:18 tells us, "they will lay hands on the sick, and they will recover." The Lord desires to use each of us to help others experience supernatural healing.

A friend of mine who serves in a prison ministry told me recently about an inmate who is part of his Bible study. He explained, "This man had a fatty cyst about the size of a large marble on his hand. When he asked for healing, I laid my hand over the cyst and prayed in full faith. After I was done praying, I noticed the cyst was a little smaller. He noticed it also. Encouraged, I prayed some more and could actually feel the cyst shrinking under my hand until it had shrunk to half its original size, but it did not disappear."

> Our God is a God of healing.

"Well, you can only do so much praying, commanding it to leave, and rebuking the enemy! I was at a loss of knowing what else to do at which point I decided to stop praying. I told the inmate, 'Let's continue to believe God to totally remove the cyst.'"

"Dismayed I wondered why it didn't totally disappear. I even looked at his hand at the end of the Bible study and noticed that the cyst was still there."

"My friend went on the say that two weeks later, the inmate showed him his hand. The cyst was totally gone. The inmate himself had sensed God telling him to pray about it seven times (similar to the Bible story about Naaman who was instructed by Elisha to wash in the Jordan River seven times). In obedience, the inmate prayed seven times and sometime later, he noticed his hand was completely healed. The cyst had disappeared."

REFLECTION
How can we experience supernatural healing through our lives?

Our God is a God of healing. He wants us to trust Him for His supernatural power to touch and change those for whom we pray. Remember, we do the praying and believing in faith—God does the healing!

The next six chapters are filled with wisdom and spiritual insights God has given to Kevin Kazemi and Merle Shenk. They will share many stories of our supernatural God manifesting Himself in our generation. Be encouraged as you read through the rest of this book. Expect to be changed and to experience the supernatural power of God in your life again and again!

CHAPTER 2

Experiencing the Fear of the Lord

Kevin Kazemi

From the East to the West

DAY 1

I was born on a rainy day in the second most populous city in Iran. Mashhad, known as the holy city of Iran, is located in the northeast of the country close to the borders of Turkmenistan and Afghanistan. This city is most famous and revered for housing the tomb of Imam Reza, the eighth Shia Imam. Every year, millions of pilgrims visit the Imam Reza shrine and pay their tributes to him. The meaning of Mashhad is "place of martyrdom."

I was born into a Muslim family. For the first six years of my life, I lived in a house of conflict. My mom was given into marriage to my dad as a very young girl, against her will. For many years we found ourselves in a prison of both verbal and physical abuse. This domestic violence almost caused my mom to commit suicide, but also led to our escape through the hands of human smugglers. After a couple of months of traveling and being smuggled into many different nations, we were stranded in Turkey. My mom wrote a letter to God that read: "God, if I didn't think you could help me I would never have left Iran. Yet I am so tired, God I'm tired of all this waiting. I am weak, sick and afraid. I am a broken-down boat in the midst of a great stormy sea. I have these children, God, and I need you to help me. If you cannot hear my voice, maybe you can read my letter."

The night after she wrote the letter, the smugglers came and said, "Have your boys ready because we will be leaving early tomorrow morning." I believe that God read my mom's letter and carried us safely to Stockholm, the capital city of Sweden.

Sweden quickly became home to me and my two brothers as we adapted to the culture and learned the language. My mom worked hard to provide for us. But in 1996, she found herself tired of life, suicidal and depressed. The day that she decided to end her life, Jesus appeared to her in a vision. That supernatural encounter led to her salvation.

As Jesus changed my mom's life and delivered her from the spirit of suicide, my life started to change also, but not for the better. From the age of fourteen, I had been using and selling drugs. Although I did not believe in my mom's God, she never stopped loving me and believing for my salvation. When I was sixteen years old my mother had an angelic encounter in a dream. In it, God instructed her to pray for my faith because I would travel to many nations, preach the gospel, and heal all kinds of sickness and disease. She took God at His word and prayed for my salvation for many years.

> That experience set me free from the dark chains of my past and changed the course of my destiny and life forever.

Then in 2004, I had a radical encounter with the supernatural power of God at a pastors and leaders conference. I was sixteen years old when my mom was given this dream, and twenty-two years old when I gave my life to

Christ. She had been praying and believing for my salvation for over six years. A young pastor from Armenia sensed an instruction from God to invite me to this conference. I had met this man very briefly, with my mom, one year before.

On September 26, 2004, I encountered the supernatural power of Jesus and He changed my life forever. God not only supernaturally saved me but also miraculously delivered me with one touch from all my drug addiction. I had been addicted to drugs from the age of fourteen, but from that moment until now I have had no symptoms or relapse.

At the moment of my salvation experience, Jesus filled my life with His Holy Spirit. I felt the presence of the Lord Jesus all over my body for several hours. As I was weeping on my knees because of His love and forgiveness, I started to speak in tongues even though I had no teaching about tongues nor was there anyone who laid hands on me to pray for me. That experience set me free from the dark chains of my past and changed the course of my destiny and life forever.

REFLECTION
Write down your testimony and condense it until you can say it within a two-minute timeframe.

"I will call them My people, who were not My people, And her beloved, who was not beloved. And it shall come to pass in the place where it was said to them, 'You are not My people,' There they shall be called the sons of the living God" (Romans 9:25-26, NKJV).

God's Heart for the Nations

From the moment of my salvation, I knew God was calling me to preach the gospel to the nations of the world. After studying in Bible school and seeing a great move of God in my hometown, I ended up traveling to South Africa for missions. While in Cape Town, I met my wonderful wife from the Netherlands. We both sensed a strong call to give our lives to serve on the mission field. We served many years in the continent of Africa in addition to traveling and preaching around the world.

> God loves every nation and is passionate to see every individual come to the saving knowledge of our Lord Jesus Christ.

As we began our journey into the mission field we only had one desire: to see souls saved. After ministering on many continents, we started to discover God's heart for the nations. If only we could understand God's unfailing love for every nation and individual, our approach to every individual regardless of their nationality or religion would change. I'm so thankful that the Bible does not say that God "so loved" the church or even a specific nation. His Word says, "God so loved the world that He gave His one and only begotten Son, that whoever believes in Him should not perish but have everlasting life" (John 3:16).

One morning while a missionary in South Africa, I was walking on the beach before sunrise. As I was listening to music with my iPod and worshiping Jesus, I was becoming very conscious of Christ in me. Suddenly a man ran up to me shaking and screaming, "Have you seen a woman?" I had never seen this man before and neither had I seen anyone that morning down at the beach. When I tried to find out who he was actually looking for, he explained that he was looking for a lady who just had a fight with her husband and had come to the beach to commit suicide after swallowing a whole bottle of pills. Even though I had not seen her, he begged me to help him search.

As I was running along the beach, with no idea who I was looking for, my eyes caught sight of something being washed up by the waves. I came closer and realized that this was a person—totally covered with sand. As far as I could see, there was no sign of life. As I dragged her out of the water she looked totally lifeless and felt very cold. Not knowing what else to do, I laid my hands on her and commanded in the name of Jesus for life to come back and for her body to reject every form of poison in her body. To my great amazement, her body started to shake violently. This so shocked me that I took my hands off of her. She suddenly started vomiting and a white foam came out of her mouth. About thirty minutes later the ambulance came and I was so pleased that the last thing she heard from me was the name of the Lord Jesus. She knew that God loved her enough to heal her and bring her back to life.

It brings joy to my heart when I know that God loves every nation and is passionate to see every individual—regardless of religion, race or culture—come to the saving knowledge of our Lord Jesus Christ.

Operation World ranks Iran as the fastest growing evangelical population in the world, with 19.6% believers in Christ. But I do not think this is the result of western Christianity's outreach. Many times it is a direct result of the Iranian Muslims experiencing the supernatural power of God revealed to them through dreams and visions.

I do not believe the nations of the world are rejecting Jesus, because according to the Bible He is the desire of all nations. Instead, nations are rejecting the Jesus that many in the church represent. The nations of the world are looking and longing for the reality of Jesus Christ whether they know it or not. In this hour, God is raising a generation that has an urgency in their hearts to represent the reality of Christ and the true knowledge of His life-changing love to a lost and dying world. It is time for the body of Christ to spend time in God's presence to rediscover His loving heartbeat and compassion for every nation.

REFLECTION
Explain how you can discover God's heart for the nations.

"The Lord is not slack concerning His promise, as some count slackness, but is long-suffering toward us, not willing that any should perish but that all should come to repentance" (2 Peter 3:9, NKJV).

In the next pages of this book, I write about how Jesus became real to me. I pray that the God who graced my life with His presence will do the same for you.

DAY 3

Reveal Yourself to me

Before Jesus revealed Himself to me in a personal, tangible way, I often asked myself the same question that I believe many people—even Christians—ask: "If God is truly real, why doesn't He reveal Himself to me?" Maybe as you are holding this book, you are asking the same question in your heart.

In 2005 while studying in a Bible School in Canton, Ohio, I had a strong desire for the reality of Jesus. I had only been born again for a couple of months and was very zealous and on fire for the Lord. My heart was filled with passion, yet I knew that there must be more of Him than what I was experiencing. Many times I felt frustrated because not everybody around me understood my longing. Some people said, "Kevin, stop looking for a sign." I knew that I was not looking for a sign. Neither was I looking for a dream or a vision. I was not even seeking any gifts. All I wanted was to encounter this God who had so gripped my heart with His love. As Leonard Ravenhill says in his book *Why Revival Tarries,* "Though it is wonderful indeed when God lays hold of man, earth can know one greater wonder—when a man lays hold of God."[1]

> It is my responsibility to seek and it is God's responsibility to reveal.

One day a minister from Honduras was teaching our Bible school class. Suddenly he called me out and said that

God just reminded him of the mighty evangelist by the name of T. L. Osborn. The minister told me to get Osborn's book, *Soul Winning*,[2] because God wanted to speak to me through it. At the time I did not know who Osborn was nor had I ever heard of him. I later learned that T. L. Osborn was a great evangelist from Oklahoma whose ministry was marked with signs, wonders and various miracles.

As I started to read the book, I discovered that his ministry had not started with manifestations of miracles. In the book, Osborn explained that at the age of 21, he and his wife went to the mission field. His wonderful wife Daisy with great humor explained that T. L. went to change India, and she went along to change his sheets. Six months after living among the Muslims and trying on a daily basis to convince them through discussion and arguments about the truth of the gospel of Jesus Christ, they did not see even one person converted to the Lord. The couple returned back home feeling like a total failure.

One night after returning home from India, Osborn had a four-hour visitation from Jesus Christ. As Jesus Christ appeared to him, the Word became flesh. After this encounter with the Lord, his whole life and ministry changed.

Osborn then explained the importance of encountering the Lord for ourselves as Jesus had promised according to the gospel. "He who has My commandments and keeps them, it is he who loves Me. And he who loves Me will be loved by My Father, and I will love him and manifest Myself to him" (John 14:21, NKJV).

I want to talk with you for a bit about this Scripture that has so changed and impacted my relationship with the Lord. I pray that the same Holy Spirit who made this verse real to me will do the same for you, in Jesus' name.

Jesus made a promise to His disciples that includes anyone who has chosen to learn and follow Him. The word *disciple* simply means "a learner." Jesus promised that if we obey Him by the law of love, He would manifest or reveal Himself to us. The word *manifest* means "to cause to shine, thus to appear, come to view, reveal, make visible or present oneself to the sight of another." In verse 21, to manifest means "the self-revelation of Jesus to believers." Jesus made this promise to anyone who believes in Him—the ones who demonstrate their love to Him through their obedience and commitment to His commandments.

REFLECTION
Does asking for more of God display a lack of faith? In what ways are you pursuing the supernatural?

After realizing Jesus' desire and standing on His promises, I began believing that He wanted to reveal Himself to me. I started the journey of pursuit that led me into a tangible and supernatural encounter with Jesus Christ. I will share more about this in the coming chapters.

As I continued this journey of pursuit, I discovered that it is my responsibility to seek and it is God's responsibility to reveal. I learned that we should never seek according to a prescribed formula, nor should we dictate what we want to see or how He needs to reveal Himself to us. Maybe you will or will not experience Him in the way the Lord chose to reveal Himself to T.L Osborn or to myself, but the main point is that Jesus desires to become real to you so that you can know Him intimately. Your relationship with the resurrected Jesus will make you a witness for Him to a lost and a dying world.

The Lord Jesus, in this hour, is inviting us to something more than just knowing the terminology of His kingdom—He desires that we experience the reality of His kingdom.

The True Supernatural Power of Jesus

What touched me thirteen years ago when I accepted Christ was not an empty form of godliness—but the true supernatural power of Jesus Christ. I believe that the only thing that can change this world is His supernatural power working through a generation that knows His reality. That was the key for the supernatural life of the first apostles, who had not only walked with Christ for three and a half years, but had also become firsthand witnesses of His resurrection. It is still the key for us today.

> The only thing that can change this world is His supernatural power working through a generation that knows His reality.

After my one year of Bible school in the United States, I returned back home to Sweden. I had only been a Christian for about a year and had no home church because I left

Sweden to study very soon after my salvation experience. My brothers were still not walking with the Lord and I had no Christian friends, nor did I know any Christians except my mom. During this season the Lord spoke to me to start a Bible study. After arguing with God a lot, I started my first Bible study together with my non-believing cousin and brothers. I had no experience and, to be honest, did not even know what I was doing. But the Lord through His goodness and love poured out His presence and in a very short while the group grew to almost forty. This was quite amazing, especially in a country like Sweden and in the type of neighborhood we were in. God was revealing Himself to many of us in profound ways.

At one point, I had to leave for seven days to go on a mission trip to Latvia. After returning home I received an urgent request from one of the Bible study group members to go meet with him and his girlfriend. As we were talking, his Swedish girlfriend told me that for the past seven days when I had been traveling, every single night Jesus came and stood next to her bed in her dreams. She went on to say that this was terrifying for her as the Lord would just stand there, not saying a word. She would wake up every time covered with sweat and feeling in her heart that she needed to get right with God. We prayed with her to do just that, and after that she became a regular member of our Bible study.

REFLECTION
Are there any areas of life in which God is calling you to a deeper level of obedience? If so, what are they?

This was just one of the experiences through which I learned the reward of obedience and the accompanying signs that follow the preaching of the Word of God according to Mark 16:20.

The Lord Jesus must become real to you before you can walk in the supernatural power that you so desire. If God is not real to you, you cannot truly represent Him as a living God to the people around you. Jesus must become alive in your life in order for Him to shine His light through you and for you to demonstrate His resurrection power.

Seen by Multitudes

The book of Acts opens with Jesus appearing to His disciples and giving them many unmistakable proofs about His resurrection. For forty days and forty nights the disciples saw Him face to face and listened to Him explain the kingdom of God.

"To whom He also presented Himself alive after His suffering by many infallible proofs, being seen by them during forty days and speaking of the things pertaining to the kingdom of God" (Acts. 1:3, NKJV).

Many times we read the Scriptures without stopping to think about what was actually taking place. Consider for a moment: ordinary people just like us walked, talked, ate and fellowshipped with the Lord Jesus in His resurrected body for forty days. That is absolutely mind-blowing and astonishing! Not only was He seen by the apostles, but the

Bible says that after His resurrection, He was seen by more than five hundred brethren at one occasion, and last of all He was seen by Paul the apostle.

I believe there were many more than five hundred people who saw the Lord Jesus before He ascended to heaven. For example, Paul does not mention Mary's name specifically, yet she was the first one who saw Jesus after His resurrection, according to Mark's gospel. "Now when He rose early on the first day of the week, He appeared first to Mary Magdalene, out of whom He had cast seven demons" (Mark 16:9, NKJV).

> Ordinary people just like us walked, talked, ate and fellowshipped with the Lord Jesus in His resurrected body

The omission of at least one person, Mary, indicates to me that the number five hundred might not have included women and children. The Bible specifically explains that women and children were not included in the numbering of the reported number of five thousand who were supernaturally fed by the Lord when he multiplied the five loaves of bread and two fish. It could be that the women and children are likewise not included among the five hundred brethren who saw the risen Lord.

Think for a moment. Would all of these hundreds or maybe thousands of men, women, and children who saw the Lord Jesus in His resurrected body been called to the five-fold ministry? Or were they all standing in the office of a prophet? I don't think so. Probably many of them were simply believers working in different spheres of society—like many of you who are reading this book.

James 5:17-18 (NKJV) says, "Elijah was a man with a nature like ours. He prayed earnestly that it would not rain, and it did not rain on the land for three years and six months. He prayed again, and the heaven gave rain, and the earth produced its fruit." The meaning of the words *same nature* is that He was subjected to the same passions, feelings and weaknesses as we are.

That which allowed Elijah, Moses or any other man or woman to be used by God in a mighty supernatural way, whether in the Bible or in the history of Christianity, was not their own greatness, but God's. Apart from the Lord Jesus' precious blood, we have nothing. "The Lord is the same yesterday, today and forever" (Hebrews 13:8). He is not a respecter of persons. He is willing to do again what He has done in the past, if we only dare to believe.

REFLECTION
In what ways have you experienced God's resurrection power in and through your life?

I believe that some of the greatest hindrances that keep us from a true life-changing encounter with the Lord are the theological boundaries we have set up in our own minds. Every encounter in the Scriptures is an invitation from the Lord to step out of those limitations and into His supernatural world.

Revelation 19:10 says that the testimony of Jesus is the spirit of prophecy. That means that every time you hear or read a testimony about what the Lord Jesus has done or is doing in someone's life, through your hunger and desire, you have the potential to step into the same encounter or miracle through faith by His grace. I pray that you will believe this with all your heart: The Lord Jesus is not required to, but He wants to make Himself real to you.

Unusual Expectation

During the summer of 2007, in my small apartment in Stockholm, Sweden, I awakened to the heat of the sun shining on my face and experienced an unusual expectation in my heart that I could not explain with words. I called my wife-to-be in The Netherlands and said, "Mariella, the Holy Spirit is going to visit me tonight." Amazed, she asked, "How do you know?"

"I don't know if I can explain it," I replied, "but last night I had an encounter with the presence of God in a way that I have never experienced before. I woke up in the middle of the night lying in my bed, surrounded by darkness and I started to feel the very dread of His presence as the Spirit of the fear of the Lord filled my room. I was undone under His mighty hand as His tangible presence was flowing through my body as a current of electricity. I could not move and was so afraid and filled with terror but somehow I knew that it was the fire of the Lord. Now I am expecting even more."

"When the people saw the thunder and lightning and heard the trumpet and saw the mountain filled with the smoke of His glory, they trembled with fear" (Exodus 20:18, NKJV).

> Before the rain of God's presence can come, we need His purifying fire.

Although I had just experienced a side of God that I had never known existed, I had so much peace in my heart. I knew that God was inviting me into an even deeper experience of Himself. That day I had a choice to make, similar to the choice that the nation of Israel had faced: to stay at a distance because of the dread of God's presence or be like Moses and choose to approach the thick darkness where God dwelled.

The Israelites stayed at a distance and told Moses, "'Speak to us yourself and we will listen. But do not have God speak to us or we will die.' Moses said to the people, 'Do not be afraid. God has come to test you so that the fear of God will be with you to keep you from sinning.' The people remained at a distance, while Moses approached the thick darkness where God was" (Exodus 20:19-21).

I wanted so much to experience Christ for myself instead of just hearing and reading stories about Him. I was tired of all the tradition and religion that I saw in the church. At the same time, I was hungry and thirsty to know more of Him and was determined to encounter Him, by His grace, for myself, no matter the cost.

In this hour, the true church is crying for God's supernatural power and for the revelation of His glory. Are we ready for it? Can we handle the glory of God if He truly manifests Himself to us? Or, do we first need the fire of His Spirit to do a work of holiness in our hearts?

Before the rain of God's presence can come, we need His purifying fire. We need a visitation of the Spirit and a deeper fear of the Lord before we can have a habitation of His glory. The Lord is looking for a church that can be His resting place—one that will not willfully grieve nor quench His Spirit.

> **REFLECTION**
> *How is God inviting you into a deeper experience of Himself?*

DAY 7

The Covering of His Hand

As I continue to share about my encounter with the Lord, I want you to know that I do not intend to boast about my own spirituality or spiritual experiences. Face-to-face encounters are like precious pearls that I so treasure in my heart. I am not willing to throw them before anybody unless I know that they also desire to encounter our precious Lord for themselves.

On that 2007 night in my apartment in Sweden, with a clear expectation that God was going to visit me once again, I went to bed. My heart was full of faith.

After hours of lying in the dark waiting with expectation, I grew tired and slumbered into a deep sleep. About 3 o'clock in the morning, I awoke suddenly. I heard a sound as if an entire forest on fire had entered my room and filled my apartment. "And suddenly there came a sound from heaven, as of a rushing mighty wind, and it filled the whole house where they were sitting" (Acts 2:2).

In 2 Chronicles 5:13-14 (NKJV), we read that when Solomon dedicated the temple and the ark was brought in, "The Levites who were the singers praised the Lord, saying: 'For He is good, for His mercy endures forever.' Then the house of the Lord, was filled with a cloud, so that the priests could not continue to stand and minister because of the cloud; for the glory of the Lord filled the house of God."

> Our Father God so desires to manifest Himself to us, but many times we don't believe it because we don't have a true revelation of His heart.

That particular night, I could feel the heavy weight of the glory of the Lord all over my body. I was so afraid that I tried to scream, but I had lost my ability to speak and no voice came out of my mouth just like was the case for Zacharias in Luke 1:22. I did not see His form but knew that He was standing before me and surely I heard the audible voice of the Lord as He spoke to me face to face as a man would speak to his friend (Exodus 33:11). He said, "Holy, holy, holy" over and over again.

Every time He spoke my whole body trembled at His voice. His words that echo into eternity penetrated deep into my heart. I knew that I was before a holy God who was setting me apart and calling me to live a holy life separated unto Him for His work. "But as He who called you is holy, you also be holy in all your conduct, because it is written, 'Be holy, for I am holy'" (1 Peter 1:15-16, NKJV).

By allowing me to experience the fear of the Lord, God was covering me with His hand so He could visit me. "So it shall be, while My glory passes by, that I will put you in the cleft of the rock, and will cover you with My hand while I pass by" (Exodus 33:22, NKJV).

The Lord had heard my cry. Because of His unfailing love for me, He was protecting me from Himself as He is a Holy God. Only as I allowed the fire of the Spirit to purge me could I have a deeper experience with Him. This purging in my life was not a work of my own human effort but a gift of His grace. It allowed me to see the beauty of repentance and it birthed in me a deep inward passion for purity. This brought a great desire in my life to be separated from the things of this world and wholeheartedly dedicated to Him.

Our Father God so desires to manifest Himself to us, but many times we don't believe it because we don't have a true revelation of His heart.

REFLECTION
Have you invited the fire of the Lord to purge you from compromise?

Ask Holy Spirit to give you a fresh revelation of the love of God that He has already poured out within your heart. "Now hope does not disappoint because the love of God has been poured out in our hearts by the Holy Spirit who was given to us" (Romans 5:5, NKJV).

CHAPTER 3

A Visitation from God

Kevin Kazemi

The Spirit of the Fear of the Lord

DAY 1

Again and again in the Scriptures, we see that when the glory of God came, the people of God could not handle it. Some people even died because they did not respect God's presence.

When King David brought the Ark of God to Jerusalem (2 Samuel 6:1-7, NKJV), Uzzah put out his hand and took hold of the ark when the oxen that were pulling its cart stumbled. The anger of the Lord was aroused against Uzzah, and he died there by the ark of God. Had the ark been carried on the shoulders of the priests, as directed by the Law, this incident would not have happened. Many times we mishandle God's glory because of ignorance, but other times it is due to lack of respect or reverence for His presence in our hearts.

When the church was birthed on the day of Pentecost, there was an outpouring of the glory of God. The church was birthed into the power of the Holy Spirit. Many signs and wonders were done through the apostles. As a result of God's supernatural power, great fear came upon every soul.

> We need the fear of the Lord in our lives if we desire to experience more of His glory.

Acts chapter five reports that Ananias sold some property but lied to the Holy Spirit by keeping part of the money. Peter asked, "'Ananias, why has Satan filled your heart to lie to the Holy Spirit and keep back part of the price of the land for yourself? While it remained, was it not your own? And after it was sold, was it not in your own control? Why have you conceived this thing in your heart? You have not lied to men but to God.' Then Ananias, hearing these words, fell down and died" (Acts 5:3-5). The same happened to Ananias' wife who walked in after him. "Because of this, great fear came upon all the church and upon all who heard these things" (Acts 5:11).

The word *holy* means "set apart." There was such a dimension of the glory of God being revealed as God laid the foundation for the New Testament church, that a great level of holiness was required. If we want the power of the New Testament church, we also need to sanctify our hearts, or in other words, we need to make a decision to set ourselves apart for God. "But sanctify the Lord God in your hearts, and always be ready to give a defense to everyone who asks you a reason for the hope that is in you, with meekness and fear" (1 Peter 3:15, NKJV).

Every time we see a greater manifestation of His glory, we also see a greater dimension of the Spirit of the fear of the Lord coming upon the church. We need the fear of the Lord in our lives if we desire to experience more of His glory.

> **REFLECTION**
> *Are there ways you can handle God's presence with respect and honor? Why is it important to do so?*

DAY 2: Delighting in the Fear of the Lord

Isaiah 11:2 identifies seven distinct ministries of the Holy Spirit that operated in the life of Jesus. One of these is the Spirit of the fear of the Lord. In Isaiah 11:3 we see that Jesus' "delight is in the fear of the Lord."

Have you ever wondered how our Lord Jesus could find His delight in the fear of the Lord? What knowledge or experience was it that He had with the Father heart of God? How could He walk in that reality continuously? I have meditated on these questions many times, and I would like to share some of the understanding that the Holy Spirit has given me about this.

It is very hard for us to truly know Him and find our delight in the fear of the Lord if we do not have a true understanding of His goodness. Many times we have a wrong picture about our heavenly Father's heart because of broken images that could be due to painful experiences with our earthly parents.

> One of the primary reasons for Jesus coming to this earth was to reveal the Father heart of God.

As we read the Gospels, we discover that one of the primary reasons for Jesus coming to this earth was to reveal the Father heart of God. He came to restore the relationship that was lost in the garden when mankind fell into sin. I am convinced that Jesus, as a Son, lived in perfect union with His Father. He had a clear revelation of His Father's heart.

Because of this understanding, He walked free from the fear of man and had His delight in the fear of the Lord.

Have you ever asked God to reveal His goodness to you? Do you desire to know the nature and the character of God? I have come to experience His unfailing and unchanging love through His goodness as He has shown me the road map to His heart. Did you know that there is a path to His heart that we can walk on just as Moses did?

Unfortunately, many of us do not, simply because we have neither an interest in knowing His heart nor a desire to seek understanding into the nature and the character of our heavenly Father.

Romans 2:4 (NKJV) asks, "Or do you despise the riches of His goodness, forbearance, and longsuffering, not knowing that the goodness of God leads you to repentance?" Only the goodness of God produces a genuine continual repentance and true repentance leads us to delight in walking the highway of the fear of the Lord. "Blessed is everyone who fears the Lord, who walks in His ways" (Psalm 128:1, NKJV).

REFLECTION
What is the difference between being afraid of God or walking in the fear of God?

DAY 3

The Path to Knowing God's Goodness

In Exodus 33, we find a man by the name of Moses who became a friend of God. The way God chose to interact with this man was different than any other person who had ever walked this planet after the fall. God said, "Hear now My words: If there is a prophet among you, I the Lord, make Myself known to him in a vision; I speak to him in a dream. Not so with My servant Moses; He is faithful in all My house. I speak with him face to face, Even plainly, and not in dark sayings; And he sees the form of the Lord" (Numbers 12:6-8, NKJV).

Moses was a man who had experienced the power of God in an amazing way, but something deep inside of him cried out for more. We see the Lord speaking to Moses face to face as a man speaking to his friend (Exodus 33:11) and Moses making a request through his friendship with God: "Now therefore, I pray, if I have found grace in Your sight, show me now Your ways, that I may know You" (Exodus 33:13).

> Moses experienced God's goodness and received a revelation of the intimate knowledge of the person of God.

Can it be that we cannot truly know God if we do not know His ways? One day I asked God this question: "Why does the Bible say in Psalm 103:7 that You made known Your ways to Moses, Your acts to the children of Israel?" God simply replied that it was because Moses asked, and the children of Israel did not. Moses found a way to God's heart that the nation of Israel never did. Moses experienced God's goodness and received a revelation of the intimate knowledge of the person of God. Today we can apply Moses' example to our lives. We can ask God and expect to receive a revelation of His goodness through the fear of the Lord.

A Visitation from God

The Holy Spirit spoke to me and said, "Kevin, if you desire to walk as Jesus walked and to live in the same dimension of God's glory, you need to allow the fear of the Lord to work in your heart and learn to have your delight in it."

When we have a revelation of God's goodness, we know that His intention is not to make us afraid, but to bring us into a greater level of intimacy. His desire is not terror but love. If His desire is a love relationship that will never be broken, then I will gladly welcome the fear of the Lord into my life and have my delight in it. I can honestly say this journey of love has not always been easy, for I have failed Him many times. In my ignorance, I have not always honored His presence.

REFLECTION
What are some of the ways we can come to know the nature and character of God?

The more I grow in the Lord, the more I am learning to have my delight in the fear of the Lord. I know it's all about a love relationship with a Holy God. My daily prayer is "Lord, help me to jealously guard and honor Your presence in every aspect of my life and help me to never lose sight of your goodness that is found in your love."

He has Heard your Cry

DAY 4

Perhaps you are saying, like many people I meet around the world, "Kevin, I desire to present the true knowledge of Christ to those around me. I can sense in my heart that there is more to this Christian life and I desire to experience more of God, but I do not know how to make that happen."

Be assured that your desire can be fulfilled. God has seen and heard your cry. The truth is that He is the one who put that desire inside of you and He is eager to answer your prayer.

Nevertheless, you can't reveal Him to the world unless He has first become real to you. As you open your heart for what the Holy Spirit wants to do in your life, you will be changed. If you long deep in your heart to encounter His manifest presence, see His face and become a resting place for Him, then welcome the Holy Spirit to examine your heart to see if there are any spiritual strongholds or any unbelief holding you back.

> Welcome the Holy Spirit to examine your heart to see if there is any unbelief or spiritual strongholds that are holding you back.

The desire of our Lord to reveal Himself to you and through you is far greater than your desire to be used by Him. He has promised that when you search for Him with all your heart, He will be found by you and reveal Himself to you.

"And you will seek Me and find Me when you search for Me with all your heart" (Jeremiah 29:14, NKJV).

If you desire to go deeper in your relationship with God and live a life filled with supernatural encounters, then put down this book for a couple of minutes to pray. Say "yes" and welcome His purifying fire to burn away any dross in your heart. "Blessed are the pure in heart, for they shall see God" (Matthew 5:8).

A Visitation from God

Yield yourself to Jesus. He has come to purge you so that you can worship Him in righteousness. If you have fallen into sin, repent and return to the Lord for He will always be there for you. Welcome the Spirit of the fear of the Lord, for by Christ's grace and love, the Holy Spirit makes you pleasing and acceptable to God so that you can present your body a living sacrifice.

REFLECTION
What are some things in your life that keep you from the supernatural?

"I beseech you, therefore, brethren, by the mercies of God, that you present your bodies a living sacrifice, holy, acceptable to God, which is your reasonable service" (Romans 12:1, NKJV).

The Time of Visitation

Throughout the summer of 2007, I continued to experience visitations from the Lord. Late one evening, while visiting my fiancé in the Netherlands, I received a phone call from a person who is dear to me who gave news that was extremely devastating and heartbreaking. I felt as if everything around me came crashing down. I had absolutely no control over this situation; neither could I be of any help as this person was on the other side of the world at the time. I felt very angry, sad and disappointed. At midnight as we walked around the neighborhood of her parent's house, I turned suddenly to Mariella and said, "I know Jesus will take care of this unjust situation."

As soon as I said these words, I looked up at the heavens and saw a star falling from the sky. Maybe this is something that is not so unusual for you, but for me, it was. Until this point, every time someone said that they saw a star falling from heaven, I was always the person who missed seeing it even though I would look up immediately. But this night, as I said, "Jesus will take care of the situation," I saw a star fall from heaven. Little did I know that this was more than just seeing a falling star—this was a time when heaven came down to earth.

> If you truly gain sight of Jesus, you will lose sight of yourself.

After returning to the house, I said good night to Mariella and went into my bedroom, locking the door after me. As I lay down in my bed, I felt very anxious, but I heard the Holy Spirit speaking to me to meditate on the faithfulness of God. Then I fell into a deep sleep.

In the middle of the night, I awoke feeling an unusual sense of the manifest presence of the Lord Jesus. On the left side of my bed, I saw a person standing in the form of a man. I was shocked and astonished because I knew I had locked the door. Sensing the holy presence of God, I realized this was not a vision nor a mental picture—this was an appearing, just like what Jacob experienced when he had wrestled with the angel of the Lord.

Have you ever wondered how real heaven can become to you? Do you have a desire for heaven to come down on the earth? The western world often finds it so hard to believe that the same Lord Jesus we worship, pray to and are in love with actually desires to become real to us.

For the first time, I understood why the Scriptures often record that when the Lord or an angel appeared full of glory to a person, the individual was afraid or fell as a dead man. "And when the disciples heard it, they fell on their faces and were greatly afraid" (Matthew 17:6, NKJV).

I, too, became afraid and did not want to look at Him. Even when I closed my eyes I could still see His appearance full of glory and truth.

Suddenly the figure walked to the edge of my bed and placed two fingers on my forehead. As His fingers touched my forehead, I felt the peace of God that surpasses all understanding fill my whole body. All of the worry, anger and anxiety that I felt before going to bed totally vanished in His presence. If you truly gain sight of Jesus, you will lose sight of yourself. I have come to discover through personal experience that many times when the Lord visits us, He comes at a time when we expect it the least but when we need it the most.

As His hand moved from the top of my head to the soles of my feet, I saw the Lord was dancing and rejoicing over me as is described in Zephaniah 3:17 (NKJV): "The Lord your God in your midst, the Mighty One, will save;

He will rejoice over you with gladness, He will quiet you with His love, He will rejoice over you with singing."

The words *rejoice over you* literally mean "to dance, skip, leap, and spin around in joy." Rejoice is translated from a Hebrew word that *Strong's Concordance* defines as "a primitive root; properly to spin around under the influence of any violent emotion, that is, usually rejoice, be glad, joy, be joyful, rejoice."[1] So Zephaniah 3:17 is more accurately translated as "Yahweh your God in your midst, the Mighty One, will save; He will rejoice over you with gladness, He will quiet you with His Love, He will dance over you with singing."

REFLECTION
How is the Lord rejoicing over you in this season of your life?

The gospel of John 1:14 (NKJV) says, "the Word became flesh and dwelt among us and we beheld His glory the glory as of the only begotten of the father full of grace and truth." In other words, there are times when the Word of God manifests itself in this natural realm. The supernatural becomes natural and the invisible becomes visible and that which is not logical becomes logical. God Himself performs it, and makes Himself and His power real to us.

Invisible becoming Visible

During the time of my visitation from the Lord, His hand continued to move from the top of my head to the sole of my feet. Soon, I felt a desire to reach out and touch

His hand. As His hand came near to mine, I reached out and grabbed it. My left hand clasped His right hand—I was holding the hand of my risen Lord! Suddenly, just as quickly as He had come, He disappeared from the room.

Lying totally still, undone and shocked by His lingering presence, I thought of the words of John, the disciple of the Lord Jesus. In 1 John 1:1 (NKJV) John said, "That which was from the beginning, which we have heard, which we have seen with our eyes, which we have looked upon, and our hands have handled, concerning the Word of life." In other words, John was testifying concerning his Lord whom he had heard, seen and touched after His resurrection. John was not talking about a Jesus who was in the grave, but about His risen Lord. John and all the other apostles including Paul became first-hand witnesses because they had a personal encounter with the risen Lord.

> The Word of God is the final authority over our lives and our experiences.

This not only happened to the disciples, and to Jacob when he was given the name Israel, but also to Abraham when the Lord appeared to him with two angels before the destruction of Sodom. "Then the Lord appeared to him by the terebinth trees of Mamre, as he was sitting in the tent door in the heat of the day. So he lifted his eyes and looked, and behold, three men were standing by him; and when he saw them, he ran from the tent door to meet them, and bowed himself to the ground" (Genesis 18:1-2, NKJV).

In Genesis 18:17, the Lord said, "Shall I hide from Abraham what I am doing?" Later we see that the Lord came and stood before Abraham and spoke to him face to face about the destruction of Sodom and Gomorrah.

I have always wondered about the reality of the supernatural in Abraham's life. How can it be possible that a mortal man can have such a relationship with an immortal God?

And it was not only Abraham. From the book of Genesis to the book of Revelation, we see many times when God appeared in different ways to His people. "God, who at various times and in various ways spoke in time past to the fathers by the prophets" (Hebrews 1:1, NKJV). Our God is a God of variety.

A supernatural visitation never contradicts the Scriptures, but always agrees with the written Word of God. Too many times we try to dictate what God can or cannot say to us based on our own personal theology and experiences. We need to realize that neither our life nor our experience is the final authority regarding the Word of God. On the contrary, the Word of God is the final authority over our lives and our experiences. God's Word should never realign itself with our lives but we should always realign our lives with His Word.

> **REFLECTION**
> *Explain what kind of relationship Abraham had with God.*

A Visitation from God

The Power of God

DAY 7

After this encounter with Christ, everything in my life changed. As I stood up, I felt as if I had been born again all over again. I am always in amazement about God's amazing grace and love for humanity. I don't understand why He loves us so much but my prayer is "Lord, give me a revelation of your love that surpasses all understanding."

Even now my heart is filled with joy as I consider how God desires to be personally involved in our lives. As stated previously, we should never seek a formula about how God will work nor should we dictate what we expect to see and how He needs to reveal Himself to us. Instead, it is our responsibility to seek Him with our whole heart and it is His responsibility to reveal Himself to us in whatever way He desires.

> Paul determined not to know anything among them except Jesus Christ and Him crucified.

The visitation is only a byproduct. The main goal of revelation, according to Ephesians 1:17, is always "about the knowledge of our Lord Jesus Christ." Our goal in life should always be to become more in love with our Lord. He is the Spirit of prophecy, He is the reason we desire visitation. It is all about the Lord Jesus.

It is so important to encounter the Lord Jesus so that He becomes real to you and is more than just a theological understanding or a form of godliness. When that encounter takes place, your life will be filled with joy and faith beyond imagination. I am convinced that only when Jesus is real to you can you truly represent the knowledge of Jesus Christ to those around you with a demonstration of His love and power.

After his powerful encounters with the risen Lord, Apostle Paul was filled with a passion to bring the people of Corinth into a personal encounter with the power of the Holy Spirit. In 1 Corinthians 2:1-5 (NKJV), the Apostle Paul said: "And I, brethren, when I came to you, I did not come with excellence of speech or of wisdom declaring to you the testimony of God. For I determined not to know anything among you except Jesus Christ and Him crucified. I was with you in weakness, in fear, and in much trembling. And my speech and my preaching were not with persuasive words of human wisdom, but in a demonstration of the Spirit and of power, that your faith should not be in the wisdom of men but in the power of God."

REFLECTION
How is the wisdom of man different from the revelation and power of God?

When Paul says that he did not come with excellence of speech or of wisdom declaring the testimony of God, he did not mean that he did not possess God's wisdom or that he did not understand the Scriptures. Instead, he determined in his heart not to depend on his human wisdom. He determined not to know anything among them except Jesus Christ and Him crucified.

Paul's message of the cross had been rejected by the philosophers in Athens because of human arguments. He discovered that no man would come to the full knowledge of the cross through an argument that comes through the wisdom of men. He even went on further to say in 1 Corinthians 1:17 that Christ had sent him to preach the gospel, not with wisdom of words, lest the cross of Christ should be made of no effect.

CHAPTER 4

Being Changed by His Presence

Kevin Kazemi

Encountering the Supernatural

DAY 1 — A Demonstration of God's Power

One evening when I was ministering in a healing meeting in the United States, I stopped and told people not to wait for me to lay hands on them, but to reach out in faith and touch the hem of Jesus' garment. In the back of the church was a lady who had a long time problem with one of her shoulders. She had gone through months of therapy for a rotator cuff injury in her shoulder and now needed surgery. As I made the statement about touching the hem of His garment, she suddenly saw a vision of the Lord Jesus with a beautiful garment standing in front of her. As she reached out to touch the hem of His garment, Jesus looked back and said to her, "Not now." She found this to be very confusing.

> God desires to demonstrate His power through us!

Then she heard me make an invitation for all those who needed healing to come to the front. She came forward and I prayed for her. She later said that as I prayed, she had felt nothing and she went back home still having pain in her shoulder. At her next appointment with her therapist, as he put his hands on her to begin the treatment, she felt a sudden infusion of the power of God touching her body—and all pain left instantly. She jumped up and lifted up her hands, praising God and saying that she was healed.

The Roman Catholic therapist could not understand what was going on, but after examination, he realized that

Being Changed by His Presence

God had performed a miracle. The rotator cuff injury was healed. This miracle became such a testimony to him that the next Sunday he was in church testifying about the goodness and the power of Jesus Christ.

I personally believe that the reason Jesus told this woman "not now" was because He wanted the therapist to also experience His reality and goodness.

God desires to demonstrate His power through us! Can it be that many times we are causing the cross of Christ to be of no effect because we try to declare the power of God with human wisdom? May we as the church of the living God bring people into an encounter with His presence and not gather people to hear our own human wisdom.

> **REFLECTION**
> What is the main reason for the spirit of wisdom and revelation according to Ephesians 1:17?
> (to know Him better)

DAY 2

God's Presence brings Healing

I was ministering at an open-air crusade in a sports stadium that was organized by a Christian radio station in a South Africa city. This city was about a five-hour drive from our home in Cape Town. On the last day of the crusade as I was ministering to the sick, I heard the Holy Spirit say to me that there was a lady with cancer in her stomach and the condition was preventing her from having children.

As I called out this word of knowledge a lady came down the stadium steps and walked directly to me through the crowd. As I looked at her I understood that this situation was very devastating in her life. As she was weeping I laid my hands on her and commanded the cancer to shrink and die, in the name of Jesus. At that moment she fell to the ground and I could truly feel an anointing of the Holy Spirit leave from my hands into her body. It was a tangible presence. We can see an anointing of power leaving Jesus in Mark 5:30 when a woman with the issue of blood for twelve years touched His garment.

> There is real power in the name of Jesus Christ! He is still doing the same miracles today that He did when He walked the earth.

Several days later a good friend of mine told me that the lady I prayed for, a relative of his, had ovarian cancer and had been told she could never have any more children. Yet she so desired to have another child. My friend went on to tell me that she had gone to the doctor after the crusade. After many examinations and with great amazement, the doctor informed her that every trace of cancer in her ovary was gone and that she could have children again.

In 2014, I was in a town in northeastern Ohio and requested by a family to pray for their 2-year-old son, Weston. He had been diagnosed with vitiligo, a non-curable skin disease that led to mysterious loss of pigmentation on his left arm.

When his parents first noticed the condition on his arm, they expected to be told that it was being caused by a fungal disease or possibly dermatitis. The diagnosis of vitiligo was such a shock to them that they sought a second opinion from another doctor, but the same diagnosis was confirmed.

This was a disease that was expected to continue and worsen. The second doctor explained to Weston's parents how stress and injuries, such as the boy falling off his bike and scraping his knee, or even being openly exposed to the sun for more than fifteen minutes, would be common triggers for new outbreaks. She prescribed topical steroids that were to be applied immediately to any new outbreak in the hope that catching it early would make the pigment loss less severe. The steroid was to work as a calming agent against inflammation on the outbreak.

Weston's mother explained to me that with every fall or stressful moment their toddler experienced, they would literally do a complete body check all over Weston's body. She recounted how they needed to adjust the lighting on several occasions when their eyes would seem to play tricks on them as they began to think that they were seeing new patches of the disease emerging from nowhere. This was both overwhelming and exhausting. When we met, this family was much in need of relief. They needed a miracle.

Despite the trauma, however, Weston's mother was full of faith. As a recourse, she had immersed herself in the

Scriptures, studying every miracle that Jesus had performed. She read online posts and testimonies of God's miracles today. At one point she told God, "You healed these people I read about, and you are the same God today that you were then. I know I can trust in you and seek solace. Weston can and will be healed, regardless of what the world says."

They continued to pray and lay hands on Weston often. Every night while he slept, every time the steroid was applied, every quiet moment, every time she simply touched him, Weston's mother would declare that God was healing him. She even spoke boldly to her young son and told him out loud that God was working a miracle in his life. These are statements that Weston remembers to this day.

Before we met, Weston's parents had decided to stop the steroid cream treatments prescribed by the doctor because they had not brought any sign of improvement. They were desperately depending on God and God alone to bring the healing; they knew very well that a miracle was needed.

Upon request, I visited their home to pray for and lay hands on Weston. We prayed together with his family, and at that very moment we could literally feel the power of God at work. Weston had been healed. From that time, the pigmentation loss did not spread a single centimeter.

After our prayers, Weston's mother continued to stand in faith, not only for progression of the disease to stop, but for it to be reversed. She asked God to go one step further and restore the pigment in Weston's arm so that no one could say in his or her unbelief, "Look at his arm, he has vitiligo. It is just dormant now."

Within two weeks, they started to notice brown freckles emerging in the white patches of Weston's arm. His pigment was returning! Before long, people around them were able to visibly see the improvement. All glory be to God!

One year later Weston returned for a follow up appointment to the doctor who had given the first diagnosis. After examining Weston's arm, the doctor grabbed his chair to have a seat. He was completely speechless. The vitiligo and its symptoms were completely gone.

> **REFLECTION**
> *When have you experienced the power of God to heal?*

There is real power in the name of Jesus Christ! He is still doing the same miracles today that He did when He walked the earth in the flesh.

DAY 3
The Kingdom of God is Within Us

After my encounter with holding the Lord's hand back in 2007, the Holy Spirit told me during a time of prayer to stretch forth my hand. As I did, He asked me this question: "Kevin, do you know why the kingdom of God is at hand?" I said that I did not. He said, "It's because you can touch it with your hand. Kevin, the kingdom of God is within reach."

The Holy Spirit reminded me of the words of Lord Jesus to the Pharisees who asked Him about the coming of the kingdom. Jesus said, "The kingdom of God does not come by observation, neither will they say it is here nor will they say it is there, for the kingdom of God is within you" (Luke 17:20-21). He was not talking about a physical kingdom but a spiritual kingdom that would exist in His people through the indwelling of the Holy Spirit after His resurrection.

> God wants to touch the world through His supernatural power and love.

I am a firm believer in the second coming of Christ according to 1 Thessalonians 4:16-17 (NKJV), "Because the Lord Himself will descend from heaven with a shout, with the voice of an archangel, and with the trumpet of God and the dead in Christ will rise first. Then we who are alive and remain shall be caught up together with them in the clouds to meet the Lord in the air. And we shall always be with the Lord."

Although my heart is anchored with hope for that day, I am not living my life waiting to be rescued from a world that is broken and dark. Jesus Christ in the fullness of His kingdom has chosen to dwell inside of us through the person of the Holy Spirit. Because He has chosen to make us His permanent home, we have become His dwelling place. According to Hebrews 6:5, we can taste the powers of the age to come.

I believe the time is coming and is already here in which we as the church no longer believe we must be in heaven before we can experience the fullness of Jesus Christ. Yes, we should be ready every day as faithful servants who are waiting and watching for our Master. We no longer need to simply survive until the rapture, for the kingdom of God is at hand. Because the kingdom of God is within us, God brings heaven to earth, which is the will of God according to the Lord's prayer which He taught His disciples as recorded in Luke chapter 11.

Jesus does not want us to wait to go to heaven, but to learn how to live now as if heaven is on earth. I remember that Pastor Dan Mohler once said, "The Lord did not only die for you to go to heaven, but for heaven to come into you." If heaven is inside of us, we have daily opportunity to release the kingdom that is within us. God does not want us to contain Him but have rivers of living water flowing out of us from our innermost being to those around us. God wants to touch the world through His supernatural power and love, but He can only do it through His body, the church. We are the church of the living God.

REFLECTION
Though we believe in the coming kingdom, why is it important to experience the Kingdom of God

Good Stewardship is Everything

In Colossians 1:25, Paul said that he became a minister according to the stewardship from God which was given for him to fulfill the Word of God. Paul continued to write about the mystery, which had been hidden from ages and from generations, but has been revealed to His saints, those who believe in Him. "To them, God willed to make known the riches of the glory of this mystery among the Gentiles: which is Christ in you, the hope of glory. Him we preach, warning every man and teaching every man in all wisdom, that we may present every man perfect in Christ Jesus" (Colossians 1:26-28, NKJV).

Paul understood that God had entrusted him with a mystery that had been hidden, but was now revealed. That ministry was not a theology nor a building nor an organization. Paul said clearly in Colossians 1:27 that the mystery is Christ in us. Christ is our hope and Christ is the glory. In other words, Paul's ministry was about stewarding Christ's presence in his life, which is the hope of God's glory to us and to the world.

> I believe that the greatest ministry and calling anyone can receive from God is to steward His presence.

When you begin to understand that the kingdom of God is within you, through the indwelling presence of the Holy Spirit, you realize that in order for you to manifest God's kingdom you need to become a good steward of His presence. The only way we can become a good steward of His presence is to learn to be continually conscious of His presence. For that to happen, your relationship with God needs to be the number one priority of your life and ministry. It is very important for us to be good stewards over everything that God has entrusted into our care. But more than just our families, churches and finances, I believe that many times we are slack in regard to stewarding the very key to everything in this life—the presence and the person of the Holy Spirit.

I believe that the greatest ministry and calling anyone can receive from God is to steward His presence. When I discovered this, and made it my number one priority and task, I literally started seeing a greater manifestation of His glory and power in my life and ministry. The more we are conscious of the Holy Spirit's presence within us, the more His power is manifest through us. The more we spend time in His presence, the more Christ within flows through us with glory and power.

God does not only want to visit us occasionally and manifest His presence now and then. He wants to live permanently within us.

After the Lord Jesus made the promise to His disciples that He would reveal Himself to the ones who love and obey His commandments (John 14:21), Judas (not Iscariot) said to Him, "Lord, how is it that You will manifest Yourself to us, and not to the world?" Jesus answered and said to him, "If anyone loves Me, he will keep My word; and My Father will love him, and We will come to him and make Our home with him" (Luke 14:22-23, NKJV). This statement is very important for us to understand. The Lord Jesus did not refer to a house but to a home. Why did the Lord Jesus say that He wants to make His home in us?

As a traveling minister, I stay in many different places. I have entered into many houses throughout the world, but have not entered many in which I truly feel at home. Recently, I ministered in a church in Bend, Oregon that is part of DOVE International and was hosted by a family in the church. This family had served in the Middle East as missionaries and had a tremendous heart of hospitality. As soon as I put my foot in their house, I no longer felt that I was a visitor who had been given a room to sleep in, but I felt that I was part of the family and completely welcome in their home.

A host with a true heart of hospitality will organize everything thoughtfully so that guests will truly feel at home. In a similar way, if we desire more than just a visitation from the Lord—if we desire a habitation of His presence—we need to learn how to be a good host.

REFLECTION
In what ways do you experience God's presence in your life or ministry?

In John 1:32 NKJV, John bore witness, saying, "I saw the Spirit descending from heaven like a dove, and He remained upon Him." The word *remain* is rendered in other translations as "he rested upon Him." In other words, Jesus had learned how to become a resting place for the Spirit of God.

If this is your desire, pray, "Lord teach me how to become the place where the soul of your feet can find rest. Amen."

Being Changed by His Presence

His Presence will Change You

DAY 5

As I have been learning to be a resting place for His Spirit, I find that I am becoming more aware of His presence daily. I believe this is the key to becoming an effective witness for the Lord.

After a season of spending time in His presence, I was flying to the Netherlands from Stockholm, Sweden. On the way to the airport, I met a young man on the bus. At first, I did not want to sit next to him because I preferred to be by myself so I could continue spending time in God's presence. As I walked to the back of the bus, I sensed God say, "Kevin, I want you sit next to that young man." I argued a bit, but I decided to obey.

As I sat down next to the young man, he turned toward me and asked where I was from. I told him that I was born in Iran. A huge smile spread across his face as he said that he also had been born in Iran. We continued our conversation talking about many things. Occasionally, he would look at me and say, "There is something different with your face." At first, I didn't understand what he was referring to but after a while, I understood what he was seeing.

> The more we spend time in God's presence, the more His nature is reflected on us.

I realized that all those days, weeks and months of spending time in God's presence had affected my countenance. That is what happened when Moses had spent time in God's presence on Mount Sinai. The Bible says in Exodus 34:29 that when Moses came down from the mountain with the two tablets of the testimony in his hands, he did not realize that the skin of his face shone with the glory of God.

I believe that the more we spend time in God's presence, the more His nature is reflected on us. We need to ask ourselves how much capacity we have as mere humans to receive and manifest the glory of God.

After the one-hour bus ride, we arrived at the airport. The young man asked if I wanted to eat lunch together before our flight. Although I preferred to head straight for the gate, I accompanied him to lunch. Abruptly he announced, "Kevin, a couple years ago I radically committed my life to Islam, and I am a follower of the prophet Muhammad."

I looked at him and replied, "A couple of years ago I radically committed my life to Christianity, and I am a follower of the Son of God, Jesus Christ."

The young man looked totally shocked as he asked in amazement, "How can you be a follower of Jesus when you are from Iran? You are supposed to be a Muslim, not a Christian."

I explained, "At a time in my life when I was drowning and no one stood by me, Buddha did not help me. Krishna did not rescue me. The prophet Muhammad did not save nor deliver me. Had they answered when I cried for help, I would have followed them, but they didn't.

REFLECTION
In what ways have you allowed God's love to touch those around you?

The one who answered and delivered me is Jesus Christ the Son of the living God. He changed my life, and I will follow Him for the rest of my life."

DAY 6 What Shall I Do to be Saved?

Our conversation with my new Iranian friend continued as we had lunch. After I declared that Jesus Christ had changed my life, he looked amazed. "Can you feel His love?" he asked.

"I don't just know God is love, I can feel His love and acceptance in my life," I explained.

"So are you saying that you have a relationship with God?" he asked.

"Yes, that is exactly the reason Jesus Christ came to the earth. He came to restore a lost and a broken humanity and bring them back to the Father God."

"Can you please tell me about this relationship?" he asked.

For an hour I told him about my love relationship with my heavenly Father. The Iranian was absolutely silent the whole time I talked, but was shaking from the presence of God.

We boarded the airplane and ended up being assigned seats next to each other; that was a miracle of its own. Inside the plane, I started sharing the gospel. Suddenly he threw his hands up and asked in front of the two female flight attendants who were sitting opposite us, "What shall I do to be saved?"

Now I was astonished. I had not even finished sharing the gospel. I knew this was a divine appointment between a lost son and his heavenly Father. I explained that we don't have to be in a certain place or in a church building, but right then, we could pray and ask God to fill his life with the same love with which He had filled mine. As we clasped hands and prayed, I saw the countenance of this young man change as God's presence filled his life. With tears in his eyes, feeling God's love and presence, the young man said, "This is absolutely amazing. I feel something like fire all around my body."

> I knew this was a divine appointment between a lost son and his heavenly Father.

As we stepped out of the airplane, the Iranian asked me if I had a Bible written in Farsi, which is our native language. I had one at home, and I would have taken it along with me had I known what was going to happen that day. However, without having a Farsi Bible to give him, we exchanged phone numbers and went separate directions.

About a month later, I again made plans to fly to the Netherlands. Two days before my flight, the airline contacted me and said that my flight had been canceled because of technical problems. Instead of Friday, they could put me on an earlier flight on a Thursday. I agreed. As I was busy packing, on Thursday, my phone rang. To my great amazement, the caller was the same young man who I had met the previous month on the plane. I told him that I was packing because I was flying later the same evening. He asked me which airline I would be on and what time the flight was. As I gave the information, he screamed and said, "I am flying from the same airport. I'm on the same flight and the same time. Please, Kevin, can you bring me a Bible?"

> **REFLECTION**
> *What do you remember about your salvation experience?*
> *Or, if you are not born again, what do you feel you need to do to respond to God's love for you?*

I was absolutely amazed and speechless that God so loved this young man that He cancelled and rescheduled my flight in order for His son to get a printed copy of His Word.

DAY 7: The Reality of Jesus

Another time when I was conducting a meeting in Stockholm, Sweden, a young man from a Muslim background attended our gathering. Suddenly in the middle of the meeting, he started arguing with me about my faith. He said that he could not understand why someone like me from a Muslim background could say that Jesus is the Son of God. He became very upset to the point of screaming at me and telling me that I should not be speaking that like when I was supposed to be a Muslim. He went on ranting about the fact that he did not believe in Jesus being the Son of God and that he could never deny his Muslim faith, as I had so shamefully done.

Even though his behavior was upsetting, I continued with the meeting. When we finished, I went home.

The next day as I was praying, there was a knock on my door. It surprised me because I was not expecting anyone. I opened the door to find the same young man who had publicly argued with me the day before. As I looked into his face I saw that he looked very terrified so I asked him to come in. He fell down on his knees and shared with me about a dream that he had the night before after leaving our gathering. He went on to say with tears running down his face that in his dream he saw himself standing in the middle of a room. Suddenly, a man who was dressed in a robe that was so red that it looked like it was dipped in blood appeared. He went on to say that somehow he recognized this man as the Lord Jesus Christ. He explained that as he looked at Him, he was gripped with tremendous fear. At that point in his dream, the prophet Muhammad entered, walked up to Jesus and bowed down to Him. Next, Buddha came in and bowed down to Jesus. Then Krishna and many who claimed to be God or sent by God did the same. His conclusion was, "Now I know for a fact that Jesus is the Christ, the Son of the living God."

> The world is looking for the reality of Jesus.

Being Changed by His Presence

As you continue to read this book, I want you to remember that the world is looking for the reality of Jesus. The only way we can make Him real to others is for Him to first become real to us. We can only give what we have just like Peter said, "Silver and gold I do not have, but what I do have I give you: In the name of Jesus Christ of Nazareth, rise up and walk" (Acts 3:6, NKJV).

REFLECTION
Explain why you can't give what you don't have.

CHAPTER 5

Experiencing His Presence

Merle Shenk

In the following chapters I try to capture nuggets of truth from God's Word that helped shape the foundation of my fifteen years of ministry in evangelism and discipleship. I will share some of my own encounters with the supernatural works of God—some that are deeply personal and I have not previously shared on a platform such as this. Any experience, without a foundation on the Word of God, is lacking. I will also share Scriptures that helped establish my worldview and that shifted me into a position of having faith to ask God to do things that I could never do on my own. These keys from the Word of God deeply impacted my life and strengthened my faith. — Merle Shenk

Walking with God

DAY 1

"Then He appointed twelve, that they might be with Him and that He might send them out to preach, and to have power to heal sicknesses and to cast out demons" (Mark 3:14-15).

Largely due to the influence of Dr. Jon Ruthven's writings, I am beginning to see this Scripture as one of the most central Scriptures in the New Testament. It touches on the very purpose of Jesus coming to earth.

Mark 3:14-15 reveals Jesus' purpose in coming to earth. It also defines how He interacts with us. This passage explains that Jesus restores us into active relationship with God ("that they may be with Him") and then sends us out to minister to others ("that He might send them out to preach and to have power to heal and to cast out demons").

In the beginning, God had perfect fellowship with His beloved creation. God walked with Adam and Eve in the cool of the day. There was no sin or separation, but a holy connection between God and man that fueled Adam and Eve's purpose as well as their mandate to steward the earth.

> Jesus lived among us and modeled the heart of God the Father to us.

When Satan's rebellion against God was introduced to mankind through the serpent, mankind followed Satan in disobeying God. This act introduced sin into the world. That sin also brought separation between God and mankind. Through various prophets and messengers, God communicated that He was going to send a redeemer—someone who would restore our relationship with God to what it had been in the Garden of Eden.

Jesus lived among us and modeled the heart of God the Father to us. He also gave us the example of how we as mankind should relate to God as our Heavenly Father. At the same time Jesus modeled for us how to relate to other people. In His book, *God is Good*, Bill Johnson says, "Whatever you think you know about God but you can't find in the person of Jesus, you have reason to question. Jesus Christ is the fullest and most precise revelation of the Father and His nature to ever be made known." [1]

Jesus did so much modeling while He was here on earth. If Jesus' only purpose was to die on the cross for our sins, He would not have to take thirty years to grow up and then spend another three and a half years in ministry. But throughout those years, he was modeling how to treat those who don't know Christ, how to relate to the Father, how to live a life without sin, how to experience the love of the Father, and how to work with the Holy Spirit.

In one specific ministry session, God used me to help bring deliverance from demonic influence to one of His children. During the demonic manifestation, the demon kept screaming, "I am not loved. I am not good enough."

I have seen this same type of manifestation on several occasions. This person was speaking out the lies that the demon had tempted them to believe. Receiving and believing those lies had given the enemy a foothold. Through submission to Jesus and resistance of the devil as explained in James chapter four, the power of demonic presence was broken off. This wonderful child of God began to recognize the amazing love of the Heavenly Father.

The enemy brings a voice of inadequacy, shame, guilt, fear, disgust, hatred, despair, negativity and discouragement. The Heavenly Father, however, gives words of life, hope, encouragement, freedom, endurance, love, joy, kindness, grace, peace, goodness, justice and mercy. He speaks words of truth with grace, while the enemy speaks words of partial or twisted truth that come with condemnation.

REFLECTION
Do the things you believe deep in your core agree with the voice of God, or the voice of the enemy?

Think about some of your own core thoughts and emotions regarding how you feel about yourself, how you view God, and how you view His love for you. If it helps to verbalize these thoughts or write them down, please do so. Scrutinize your own thoughts in the light of Scripture and what the Word reveals about the thoughts that God has toward you. Which voice do your thoughts align with, the voice of God or the voice of the enemy?

Let's pray and ask God to wash us of any lies that we believe consciously or subconsciously.

"Father, today I come to you in Jesus' name. I repent of any lies of believing _____ (list each thought that is in the category of agreement with the enemy). I come to you, Jesus, asking you to wash me and cleanse me of the effects of these lies. Right now, by the power of your blood I submit my mind, my body and my spirit to you. I revoke the right of any lies of the enemy to distort how I see God, myself and others, in Jesus' name. Thank you for filling me with your Holy Spirit. Amen."

DAY 2 Receiving through Time with God

"And as you go, preach, saying, 'The kingdom of heaven is at hand.' Heal the sick, cleanse the lepers, raise the dead, cast out demons. Freely you have received, freely give" (Matthew 10:7-8).

In the beginning of this chapter we read that Jesus appointed His disciples "that they might be with Him." Part of His main purpose on earth was for us, His people, to be with Him!

> This inner walk with the Lord is not preserved for only a few; it is available for every believer!

Asking God's truth to destroy any lies we believe is so important, because believing the lies of the enemy opens doors for sin and distortion in our lives. That sin can break the fellowship we have with God and it can also distort how we see other people.

In Matthew 10:7-8, Jesus further instructed His disciples, "And as you go, preach, saying, 'The kingdom of heaven is at hand.' Heal the sick, cleanse the lepers, raise the dead, cast out demons. Freely you have received, freely give."

We receive freely, and we are told to give freely in return. It is in being with the Father that we receive from Him. Our personal times with God also empower us to minister life to others. In a place of walking in relationship with God in our inner man, we are fueled and filled with revelation from His Word and with the power of the Holy Spirit. This secret place is where we receive empowered grace to accomplish the tasks that God gives to us.

Jesus speaks about this inner place. He says in Matthew 6:6, "But you, when you pray, go into your room, and when you have shut your door, pray to your Father who is in the secret place; and your Father who sees in secret will reward you openly." When Paul speaks of praying "without ceasing" in I Thessalonians 5:17, I believe he is describing the way in which our hearts can continually live in a secret place of communion with God's presence.

This inner place is a place of intimacy and secrecy with the Father. It goes far beyond a finite physical room. The secret place is something we can begin to carry with us all day, every day. It is a place of internal meditation upon the truth of God's Word, as David explained in Psalm 119:11, that he hid God's Word in his heart so he would not sin. Again the psalmist writes, "Behold, you delight in truth in the inward being, and you teach me wisdom in the secret heart" (Psalms 51:6, ESV).

When we manage our inner man by kicking out lies of the enemy, meditating on the truth of God's Word, being filled to overflowing with the Holy Spirit, and then intentionally listening to what He may say to us throughout our day, we become literal ambassadors for the kingdom of God. We can see the supernatural break into the everyday moments of our lives.

REFLECTION
Is there anything that you need to stop doing or not allow in your life because it is causing your inner life with God to deteriorate?

I believe that cultivating this continual fellowship in our inner life with God is a form of prayer.

This inner life with God is governed by what I have come to call the law of love. This law is part of the New Covenant referred to in Romans 8:2 which states, "For the law of the Spirit of life has set you free in Christ Jesus from the law of sin and death." The law of love constrains us from doing anything or allowing any thought that violates God's love for us, or ours for Him.

The law of love can be compared to a marriage relationship. I do not want to do anything that violates the love that my wife and I share. This goes beyond simply not committing the physical act of adultery. This means I will keep my imagination pure by not viewing pornography or thinking lustfully about other women. It means I will guard my heart against exclusive emotional connections and unhealthy soul ties. My greatest emotional intimacy belongs to my wife, and I will both nurture and protect that intimacy in every way that I can.

Jesus addressed the reality of adultery and hate found in the heart before condemning the actual manifestation of physical deeds. Maintaining our inner walk with God and being dedicated to what brings His life to our innermost parts, is of utmost importance for walking a supernatural life. When we entertain things that violate our love relationship with God, it chips away our intimacy with Him. If left uncorrected, our consciences can become seared to the point that we cannot hear His voice and are not able to respond in obedience to Him. This can rob people of experiencing God's working supernaturally through them.

This inner walk with God is for everybody. It is for you! It requires time and intentionality, but it is so worth it. It is necessary for those who desire to walk in the supernatural. This inner walk with the Lord is not preserved for only a few; it is cultivated by all who are willing to pursue it. The secret inner place is the place where we receive from Him.

"Father I ask that you lead us by Your Holy Spirit to guard our hearts and protect the wellspring of life that you have placed within. We want to receive from you so that we can give to others. In Jesus' name, Amen."

Moving with the Holy Spirit

"And I will pray the Father, and He will give you another Helper, that He may abide with you forever—the Spirit of truth, whom the world cannot receive, because it neither sees Him nor knows Him; but you know Him, for He dwells with you and will be in you" (John 14:16-17).

In speaking about our inner life with God, it is imperative that we speak about the role of the Holy Spirit. The Holy Spirit is not just a force, but is the means through which we live in continual connection with God. He is the Helper who Jesus says will be with us and in us.

The Holy Spirit is the one who helps us steward our inner life with God. He leads us into truth in every matter that concerns us. He is the one who makes known to us all that God has for us. He also makes known what we need to know and reveals it to us when we need to know it.

> The Holy Spirit is the one who helps us to steward our inner life with God.

I often receive words of knowledge, which is a gift of the Holy Spirit mentioned in 1 Corinthians 12. It is knowledge that we have no way of knowing naturally. One of the ways that this gift manifests in my life is through receiving timely Scripture references in my spirit that turn out to be accurate "now" words that perfectly apply to certain situations. Sometimes people marvel at what they perceive to be my extensive knowledge of Scripture; it seems to them that I can just pull up relevant and applicable Scriptures on demand. It is actually a supernatural gift, a word of knowledge given through the Holy Spirit.

After sharing a verse that accurately defined the season we were in and gave direction on how to pray, a friend of mine retorted, "It is really easy to see the problems and find a Scripture that applies." I had to laugh; I was not nearly as smart at what he was giving me credit for. I had simply received an impression of a Scripture reference but did not actually know the words in the verse. When I looked up that Scripture, the words applied perfectly. That impression from the Holy Spirit is a word of knowledge that is clearly supernatural because I know my own limitations. I have received many words of knowledge apart from Scripture references, but receiving Scriptures has been a significant part of my training from God.

I was never adept at Bible memorization as a child, and as an adult, I rarely remember Scripture references for verses that I have memorized. (It is often an Internet search that enables me to find references). Honestly, getting Scripture references in times of prayer did not come easily at first; it required a lot of practice. During my Bible school days, I was often embarrassed and frustrated by looking for reference numbers in the Bible that did not exist, but I kept with it. I learned to discern the types of impressions that were from the Holy Spirit and those that were from my own imagination or human effort.

REFLECTION
Have you invited the Holy Spirit to fill you continually?

It is the Holy Spirit who gives us what we need to know when we need to know it. He is the one who keeps us connected to God. He is the one who makes known to us all that God has for us. Everything that we need from the mind of Christ for our situations is available to us through the supernatural gifts of the Holy Spirit!

We can make a comparison with the Internet. If the Internet represents all that God the Father has for us—His plans for us according to Jeremiah 29:11, His love, presence and will—then Jesus could be compared to the router, which connects us to the Internet. The Holy Spirit is the Wi-Fi airwaves that are constantly around us in the room. When our wireless devices are "on" they are filled with the Wi-Fi waves, bringing a continual connection to all the information found on the Internet. Of course, this is just an illustration. I am not diminishing God's ability to the Internet, but the analogy might help us!

The Holy Spirit is the one who appropriates all that God has for us in our relationship with Him. The Holy Spirit is the one who keeps us connected to the Father in real time. It is through the Holy Spirit that we know and perceive what God has made available to us. As explained in 1 Corinthians 2:12, "Now we have received, not the spirit of the world, but the Spirit who is from God, that we might know the things that have been freely given to us by God."

God with You: Emmanuel

"Have I not commanded you? Be strong and of good courage; do not be afraid, nor be dismayed, for the Lord your God is with you wherever you go" (Joshua 1:9).

This Scripture has become more precious to me in the last several years. I have a wonderful family and godly parents. I happen to be the youngest of six children. Not only that, but I am six years younger than my closest sibling and there is another six years between her and my next sibling. Therefore I was very much on the "tail end" in our family, a position that has perks. My parents had become experts in child rearing by the time I came along, plus I had the huge advantage of learning from observing my older siblings.

> Supernatural signs, wonders and miracles are never a substitute for God's presence.

This birth order did mean that I spent a lot of time playing alone. When I was young, times were financially tough for everyone in our farming community and especially for my parents who had just built a new shop for their business that serviced the farming industry. After building the shop, bank interest rates shot up to 18 percent. Farmers were having difficulty paying and my dad had to work especially hard to provide for his family of eight.

In this environment I internalized the concept that life is difficult. I didn't know how serious our status was, but I knew that we were struggling just to survive. This framed my early childhood to the extent that I would play out survival situations. I would go out in thunderstorms and snowstorms to pretend I was lost and I had to survive. In my eyes, our front lawn and the woods behind our house were vast amounts of barren wilderness that needed to be survived with no hope of rescue. Well, until dinner was ready anyway!

It was a wonderful childhood, yet in all of this I developed a core internal belief that I was alone and could not depend on others to help me. Only during our missionary years did I recognize how this belief of needing to "go it alone" in times of difficulty was affecting my adult life. I preferred to handle challenging situations on my own, yet that feeling of being alone was the thing I hated and feared the most. It was affecting my spiritual life, marriage, and leadership. I did not know how to ask for the support that I needed. I did not know how to build effective teams that could support each other, or that could be a support to me.

Part of the way through our missionary experience, I went through a season of burnout, but God was still moving in the church we had planted. I would pray for people who had been diagnosed with HIV/Aids and they would come back with medical reports that confirmed healing. Significant healings were taking place on a regular basis in our small inner-city church. Yet I was frustrated and did not know how to communicate what I was feeling. I felt alone. I had believed a lie from the father of lies that I would always be alone and that I could not count on others for help. I was surrounded by people who loved me—but I still felt alone.

During this season, I realized that supernatural signs, wonders and miracles are never a substitute for God's presence. His presence and the knowledge of His love are the most supernatural things we can ever experience. Through this dark time in my life, God proved Himself to me. He proved that He was going to be there for me when I did not even know how to reach out for help. He proved that His presence was not dependent on my faith—but on His faithfulness. He was and is Emmanuel: God with us.

God orchestrated multiple divine connections and brought us out of that difficult season step by step. We began to learn how to succeed in what He had called us to do. By the time God called us back to the USA in 2016, our church was vibrant and growing, and we continued to see God do significant miracles of healing.

REFLECTION
What are ways in which you know that God is with you?

God proved Himself to me in such a way that I know beyond a shadow of a doubt that I am never alone. In that time of deep trial, I learned how to dialog fearful scenarios with Him. Even today when I am faced with the fear of speaking to a new crowd of people I ask Him, "God, I can't do this without you. I need you to have my back." Many times I hear His soft reply, "Go for it; I am with you."

His words to us are truly amazing. "I will never leave you nor forsake you" (Hebrews 13:5). It means that no matter what valleys or mountaintops we walk through, we are guaranteed to have His presence with us.

DAY 5 — Knowing the Heavenly Father

"So that you may be sons of your Father who is in heaven. For he makes his sun rise on the evil and on the good, and sends rain on the just and on the unjust. For if you love those who love you, what reward do you have? Do not even the tax collectors do the same? And if you greet only your brothers, what more are you doing than others? Do not even the Gentiles do the same? You therefore must be perfect, as your heavenly Father is perfect" (Matthew 5:45-48, ESV).

> Revealing the Father to us was one of Jesus' main purposes for coming to earth.

Revealing the Father to us was one of Jesus' main purposes for coming to earth.

As I have sought to hear what Jesus says about God the Father, I have been led to these verses in Matthew chapter five. The last verse quoted here gives us a very heavy requirement: being perfect. Is that even possible?

In this passage, Jesus is showing us that God is a completely healthy Father. The original word for *perfect* implies "whole, lacking nothing." In other words, God is complete and whole. He is not deficient in any way. He is not a dysfunctional parent who gives love in order to get love in return.

And because He is not lacking in any way, God does not need our love in order to be loving to us. He is not loving towards us because we love Him. This sounds so simple. Yet many people are afraid that if they are not good enough, God will not love them.

God's love is not a reward for our performance. It is a gift to be received! It is a product of who He is, which means that we never have to fear not being loved! We only need to fear that we could fail to receive His love, even though it is available.

As I meditated on this verse, God began to systematically dismantle a drive toward performance that I had not even realized I had. My wife, Cheree and I had given up everything to go to the mission field: our home, good paying jobs, close proximity to family and friends... we were working hard for God. Surely God saw us in a more favorable light than those who hadn't done all these things, I secretly assumed, but I was wrong.

God loves everyone equally. Jesus is saying that the way the Father loves is the same way that He makes His sun rise on the evil just as much as on the good. He loves in the same way He sends His rain. It goes to both the just and the unjust. His love for us does not change, but when we receive His love, it changes us!

I viewed my family's sacrifice as a way of performing for God. I heard it said that moving in a supernatural lifestyle can become just another way to perform. We do not want that. We must lay down any performance mentality and receive God's unconditional love.

Why is this important for living a supernatural life? The bedrock belief of God's love for us is necessary so that we also understand how deeply He loves other people. If we are so convicted that He loves us recklessly and utterly, then we will have no problem understanding that He loves someone who prostitutes themselves or someone who is addicted to drugs just as much as He loves us. He loves those who have performed abortions just as much as He loves anyone else. This empowers us to minister to others. Miracles and the gifts of Holy Spirit are simply packages that carry the love from the Father, and we are privileged to pass them out to others!

In a parable in Luke chapter 15, Jesus told of a son who was jealous of his father's love for his younger prodigal brother. May we not display that attitude! We do not want to be jealous of miracles that others receive; rather we need to bask in the joy of a loved person receiving a gift of love from our heavenly Father!

There have been times when I prayed for people and saw God move in a mighty way, and yet my family or I would at the same time be standing in need of the same miracle! In this scenario, if we have a performance mentality, we could feel insecure, doubting ourselves, or questioning why God loves that person more. A performance mentality steals our ability to joyfully celebrate when someone else gets a breakthrough.

Jesus says that we are to love others in the same way that God loves them, regardless of how they treat us or how they act.

Let's add two more verses to our Scripture reading.

"You have heard that it was said, 'You shall love your neighbor and hate your enemy.' But I say to you, 'Love your enemies and pray for those who persecute you, so that you may be sons of your Father who is in heaven. For he makes his sun rise on the evil and on the good, and sends rain on the just and on the unjust. For if you love those who love you, what reward do you have? Do not even the tax collectors do the same? And if you greet only your brothers, what more are you doing than others? Do not even the Gentiles do the same? You therefore must be perfect, as your heavenly Father is perfect'" (Matthew 5:43-48 ESV).

REFLECTION
Why is it important to receive a deep and enduring revelation of God's love for us?

I like to envision God's love as a river that is full and rushing. It is flowing in one direction, out from Him. We are to be channels of that river, giving His love to every person whether they love us in return or not. Miracles and signs then become a normal result of loving others as God loves them.

DAY 6

What Makes a Person Valuable?

"'Tell us, then, what you think. Is it lawful to pay taxes to Caesar, or not?' But Jesus, aware of their malice, said, 'Why put me to the test, you hypocrites? Show me the coin for the tax.' And they brought him a denarius. And Jesus said to them, 'Whose likeness and inscription is this?' They said, 'Caesar's.' Then he said to them, 'Therefore render to Caesar the things that are Caesar's, and to God the things that are God's'" (Matthew 22:17-21, ESV).

A coin has value because of the image that is stamped upon it. Every nation has currency with specific images and seals of that country. The government that mints its seal upon a coin is the one that determines the value of that specific denomination of currency.

> People are valuable because every person has been created in the image and likeness of God.

I remember being in Zimbabwe and holding a one-dollar bill that was so faded and dirty that it was almost unrecognizable. It was the most worn piece of money I had ever seen. Yet despite its desperate condition, it was just as valuable as a crisp new dollar bill. I think God sees people in the same way. No matter the age or revolting impression, each person is as valuable to God as the one who exhibits the most perfect appearance.

In this Scripture, Jesus underlines an important principle: that which gives a coin value and identity is the image that it bears. Jesus instructs us not only to pay taxes, but to also give to God the things that God has stamped with His image and likeness.

Value comes not from the things that people do, nor the work they produce, nor their contributions to society, nor their beauty. People are valuable because every person is created in the image and likeness of God and is worthy of respect and honor regardless of any behavior.

Often our natural inclination is to judge people according to the way they treat us or based upon what they contribute to society. God does not share this humanistic view. God does not love and value us based on what He can get out of us. Neither does He love us because He is impressed with our righteous lifestyle. The Bible says that God loved us first before we ever loved Him. That means God has an open-hearted perspective of us before we even repent. He loves and values each of us before we welcome Him into our lives.

REFLECTION
Do you treat others according to their created value?

God treats no one as they deserve. God does not reject anyone while there is still a chance for them to repent and come to Him. Neither should we judge others and dismiss them as being beyond hope of living a changed life.

Remember, the way God treats us—the undeserving—is a reflection of who He is. Sadly, the way we treat others often tends to be more of a reflection of our own attitudes than of their inherent worth.

An open-hearted embrace toward others is one of the keys to seeing the supernatural work of God flow through us to others. Recognize that each individual has intrinsic value because God has placed a measure of His own attributes within each one. This is the key to loving others. If we learn to value people regardless of how they act or what they contribute, we are closer to having God's heart for others.

Helping People become Followers

"And he made from one man every nation of mankind to live on all the face of the earth, having determined allotted periods and the boundaries of their dwelling place, that they should seek God, and perhaps feel their way toward him and find him. Yet he is actually not far from each one of us" (Acts 17:26-27).

Every person, no matter how sinful, is in some proximity to Jesus. While teaching in various schools of ministry, I often use the exercise described below to help students understand how God views people.

In the demonstration, one person stands in the middle of the room to represent Jesus; several people stand close to the Jesus figure; some stand a bit farther away and some go to the outskirts of the room.

Students are instructed to face different directions. Some face Jesus, some are slightly turned away, and some turn completely away from the person representing Jesus.

Students are then asked, "Who is a follower of Jesus?" Some say those closest to Him; others say those facing Him.

Each person is then asked to take a step in the direction they are facing. This results in some moving closer to Jesus and others moving farther away. I again ask the question, "Who is a follower of Jesus?" At this point most students agree that those who have chosen to face Jesus and move toward Him are His followers.

> The goal in ministering supernaturally to others is to inspire them to follow Jesus more closely.

I explain that every person we meet is represented in this example. There are those who are close to Jesus and are following Him. For example, those who are involved in a local church (close to the things of Jesus) and pursuing Him in daily relationship. There are also those who are close to the things of Jesus (the church), but their focus has shifted to other things. Their hearts are distracted and they are no longer following Jesus although they have not completely moved away from Him.

There are those who are a bit farther away from the things of Jesus. Perhaps they have family or friends who follow Jesus or live within access to hearing about Jesus through media. Perhaps they even attend church services occasionally. Some are interested in Jesus and are aware of their spiritual hunger for Him. They are facing Him and moving towards Him. They are following. They may not know much about God, but they are hungry and seeking. Some are aware of Jesus but are focused on other interests.

Those who stand far away represent a culture that has no representation of Jesus in it. Perhaps these people were born into families that practiced different religions or no religion at all. Some may have grown up simply uninformed or in an environment that was antagonistic toward Jesus or completely misrepresented Him. This category includes those who are facing Jesus and those who are not facing Him. Those who are facing Him recognize their spiritual hunger and are searching for truth or for more knowledge of Jesus. They may know nothing or have limited knowledge—but they are searching for Jesus nonetheless.

> **REFLECTION**
> *What can you do today to help others turn toward or step toward God?*

From this example, the definition of a follower of Jesus is someone who is literally *following* Him. As they continue to follow Him, even those who are far away eventually will draw near to God and He will draw near to them.

The goal in ministering supernaturally to others is to inspire them to follow Jesus more closely! This is God's desire. God will use your encounters with others to get their attention and help them turn to Him. When we see other people—no matter how rough they may seem or how far they appear to be from Christ—we should remember that they are still able to turn towards Him or step towards Him. No one is too far away to be reached by His love.

CHAPTER 6

Ministering with Jesus

Merle Shenk

DAY 1

The Kingdom of God is Available to Us

"And as you go, preach this message: 'Heaven's kingdom realm is accessible, close enough to touch.' You must continually bring healing to lepers and to those who are sick, and make it your habit to break off the demonic presence from people, and raise the dead back to life. Freely you have received the power of the kingdom, so freely release it to others. You won't need a lot of money'" (Matthew 10:7-9, The Passion Translation).

I love how The Passion Translation describes the present-tense nearness of the kingdom of God. It is close enough to touch! Other translations of the Bible say it is "at hand" or it has "come near to you" but these all mean the same thing. His kingdom is here now, appropriated to us by the Holy Spirit, today!

> There is so much more for us to experience in His Kingdom here on earth.

I love taking people who are trained in our schools of supernatural ministry along with me to other cultures. One such student from the USA was not even sure if miracles were real, but she was hungry for God and willing to pray. On a trip to Cape Town, South Africa, students went to the local park and were to pray for healing for people as a way to open the door for sharing the gospel. The student prayed for a teenage girl who was deaf and when she tested this girl's ears she discovered God had healed her. The student was not sure of the history of this girl and did not know how dramatic the miracle was until the girl's younger brother showed up. He was completely amazed that his sister could hear. He explained how hard it had been to communicate with her in the past and declared that she was definitely healed.

People have asked me many times why more miracles happen in Africa than in North America. I am not sure that this perception is entirely true. Certainly it isn't because God loves Africa more than Americans. The kingdom of God in Africa is the same as the kingdom of God in Europe and America. What is available in Africa is also fully available to the West.

Perhaps people are predisposed by culture to expect different things when they pray. In Africa many of my friends have no problem stepping out in faith and praying for each other, expecting miracles.

Where I am from in the USA, our culture tends to value hard work, saving and protecting what we have. As a nation, we reward calculated risk, a strong work ethic and business acumen. However, we can tend to subconsciously believe that we only truly deserve what we earn. Could this underlying belief cause people to not fully embrace the truth that God makes so much more available to us than what we deserve?

Many other cultures do not have such a prevalent performance-based mentality. For example, many Eastern cultures tend to believe that they can receive what is available and are inclined to believe, act on, and claim in faith the promises of Jesus. We must ask ourselves: "Do I want what is available or do I want what I deserve?"

I realize that I am making generalizations, so if you believe differently please do not be offended. I personally know many North Americans who fully believe the promises of God and are free from a performance mentality. There are also those I know from other cultures who wrestle with their faith. I am giving a basic example of how the norms found in the culture in which we have grown up could influence our openness to experiencing the supernatural. This affects how we obey the command "Freely you have received the power of the kingdom, so freely release it to others" (Matthew 10:8).

REFLECTION
How can you share what is available in God's Kingdom with others around you?

There is so much more for us to experience in His kingdom here on earth. Let us stretch our faith past only receiving what we may think we deserve, and recognize the depths of what God's grace is available to us!

What are We Assuming?

DAY 2

"Asked by the Pharisees when the kingdom of God would come, He replied to them by saying, 'The kingdom of God does not come with signs to be observed or with visible display, Nor will people say, "Look! Here [it is]!"

or, "See, [it is] there!" For behold, the kingdom of God is within you [in your hearts] and among you [surrounding you]'" (Luke 17:20-21, Amplified Bible).

Imagine this scene: Jesus is surrounded by Pharisees who had dedicated their whole lives to the study of Scripture as they were waiting for the kingdom of God and the Messiah to come. Jesus is now literally standing among them and telling them that the kingdom of God is in their midst—and they still miss it!

But before we become condescending towards the Pharisees, I want to ask: How many times is God doing something in our midst and we miss it? This happens to me more than I would like to admit.

The Pharisees were no doubt expecting the Messiah to show up on the scene in a different way than Jesus did. We really don't know what was in their minds, but I can guess that they probably thought the kingdom of God would defeat or overthrow the Roman kingdom. He would then honor the religious leaders who had been holding fast to the Jewish faith in the face of great trial. Israel would be led into a golden age.

Because things did not happen the way they assumed they would, the Pharisees were unable to see the very thing that they had dedicated their lives to. They could not recognize that it was unfolding right before their eyes.

Our assumptions about how God will move can really catch us unaware. One time I was on a prophetic presbytery team that was praying over church leaders in Africa. Sometimes leaders would want a specific direction or detailed revelation according to what they thought they needed to hear from God. We had to be very clear that we were there to only share what God gave us to say and were not in a position to decide what God would reveal.

Some of the leaders were offended because they did not get the specific answers that they wanted. They could not receive what God was saying to them because they were so focused on wanting to receive certain specific details.

> Our assumptions can rob us from seeing what God is busy doing in those around us.

In this setting, I also almost completely misunderstood what God was saying to one young man because of my own assumptions. As we began to pray, in my mind, I saw the young man moving on a highway. I saw a young lady who I understood to be his wife merging onto the highway from the onramp. The impression that I had was that he should continue going in ministry on the road God had called him to walk on and not be looking around for his wife. God would bring his wife alongside him at the right time as easily as an onramp brings cars onto a highway. He seemed very receptive to this word. I was careful not to share more than what I specifically saw. What happened next shocked me.

This was a young man possibly in his early twenties. I assumed from the vision that, like most young men of that age, he was looking for a wife and God was telling him that He would bring her to him as he faithfully continued in what God had given him to do. I so easily could have let this assumption influence the way I shared the word. Even worse, I could have mixed my own assumptions into what I shared with him and actually caused this word to become a wrong word. But I am so glad I did not!

After the prayer session, I casually asked this man if he was married. (It had been my assumption that he was not). When he responded that he was already married, I really panicked!

I was confused. I was so sure that what I had received was from the Lord. Had I "missed it" completely? I was afraid because I knew polygamy was still practiced in this nation. I was concerned about what this young man may have assumed from my comments. After he left, I told those on the team that I wanted to submit this word to them because it seemed that I had missed it entirely. One older minister who was a part of that team gave me wise counsel. He said that we should not jump to conclusions. He encouraged me to wait and allow the young man to define for himself what God was saying. I made one assumption already, and was almost making another one. Honestly, it took me a while before I was willing to contribute into the ministry of others for whom we were praying.

The next day I approached this young man and asked him if the word I gave him made sense. I really wanted to know. I needed the feedback, and what he said gave me great relief. He said that the word was very accurate. He explained that he had been resentful toward his wife who was not able to be with him at ministry functions because they had a young child. At times he would get up to pray at midnight and resented her for being asleep while he was praying. He felt as if she was not supportive of him in his ministry call because she was not with him all the time.

> **REFLECTION**
> *If we receive prophetic words or impressions for others, how can we make sure that we do not mix in our own assumptions when sharing them?*

God's message had clearly meant that he should continue doing what he was supposed to do and not resent his wife's apparent lack of involvement. He was not to resent her for being tired and not praying with him in the middle of the night. What was prophesied was that "God would bring his wife alongside him at the right time." So that is what he understood. I was so glad that what I shared was not being used as justification for finding another wife! The way the revelation ministered to this man was certainly not from my own mind, but God had revealed it in His unique way.

Our assumptions can so quickly rob us from seeing what God is busy doing in those around us or even blind us to see what God is doing in our own lives.

Carrying Jesus to Others

"But Jesus answered them, 'My Father is working until now, and I am working'" (John 5:17).

To minister effectively we need to find out what God is busy doing and join Him in it. The traditional picture of missions and ministry is that as ministers we are carrying Jesus into a new city or region. We are carrying Him where people do not yet know Him. In this framework, people sometimes believe that Jesus is not working in an area until they show up!

I like to see ministry a bit differently. I believe that God is already working in the places that we are going to minister. Jesus said in John 6:44 that no one can come to Him unless the Father draws him. God is busy drawing people to Himself. People are contemplating their lives deeply. They have dreams and longings in their hearts that they do not understand. All these represent different ways God uses to draw people to Himself.

People who are being drawn by the Father may simply need our testimony so they can recognize God calling them. Maybe they just need to hear the Gospel so that they can recognize that the God of the entire universe is reaching out to them. It is our testimony that helps them understand this. It is not about us getting them to say our prayer or believe our words. When they realize that God Himself is drawing them to Himself, there is no argument.

I saw this happen in a Bible study that I was leading. A young lady, new that night, was not following Jesus. Our procedure in the Bible study is for each person to share with the group one thing that they are thankful for from the previous week; this takes one minute or less per person. Then every person shares one challenge that they faced in the previous week. We pray for each other and try to help each other in practical ways if we can. Then we engage in a Bible reading where everyone participates. Based on the Bible reading, we pause to listen to what God would speak to us personally from the verses we read. Thereafter, we all share what God is saying about ourselves and make an "I will" statement, committing ourselves to a specific act of obedience as a direct response to what God has spoken to us. We end the gathering by asking God whom we can reach out to in the coming week.

> God is busy drawing people to Himself.

At the point where we were to sit and listen to what God was saying to us about us, I was cautiously optimistic with this unbeliever present. Would she receive anything from God? As it came time for this young lady to share what she felt God was saying to her in front of the group I waited with expectation. Yes, He did speak to her. Her words were, "I believe that God is asking me to come to Him." Wow. Praise God!

Because she heard God's voice for herself, there was no argument about the divinity of Jesus or the legitimacy of

His word, or a comparative discussion about why Christianity is the only way to God. None of that! I could just simply lead her to the next step which was to ask, "What will you do to obey what He is asking you?" That night, she came to Jesus and is still serving Him to this day.

> **REFLECTION**
> *What are ways that you can help others find Jesus?*

It is amazing when people hear God through His Word for themselves! It is truly amazing what people hear from the Lord, especially those who have not embraced Jesus as their Savior yet.

There is obviously more to this type of Bible study than I am discussing here. Feel free to contact me for more information if you desire. Helping people respond to God is truly amazing.

Learning to Listen

"My sheep hear my voice, and I know them, and they follow me" (John 10:27).

Revelatory gifts are the Holy Spirit gifts of prophecy, words of wisdom and words of knowledge. At a certain point in my life, the use of revelatory gifts was increasing. The more I was stepping out in faith to use these gifts, the more revelation I was receiving from the Holy Spirit. This meant, however, that I was becoming overwhelmed with everything I was receiving. Two examples will illustrate this.

The first is when I would sit down to counsel someone who was in trouble. As they began to tell the story of how they got to their place of difficulty, I would perceive a timeline of various mistakes they made, with one poor choice leading to another to another. Sometimes I would receive this by natural discernment and sometimes by revelatory gifts. Either way, seeing mistake after mistake could be so disheartening! Eventually I would get so overwhelmed that I would not know where or how to start counseling them. I wanted to give up. How do you undo twenty years of mistakes in a few simple counseling sessions?

Another example is that I would become very burdened due to sensing things in the spirit realm. When in a group of people, I would begin to pick up on various needs of people in the room. One person needs encouragement; another needs a revelation about how to treat their spouse; another is too stressed for too long. Maybe another person is struggling with insecurity and needs acceptance, and yet another needs understanding of their purpose and specific direction for their job. Someone is sick; someone else is depressed. . . and they all need prayer and ministry! The needs would go on and on.

I remember a time when I tried to respond to every need that I was discerning. At first this seemed wonderful that God was using me! It was also exhausting! I could not keep up with the needs that I was seeing and I no longer enjoyed being with groups of people.

I did not know how to steward the revelatory gifts that I was beginning to minister with. This was probably one of the factors that contributed to the burnout that I experienced around that same season of life.

My main problem was that I thought I was responsible for every ministry need that I saw! I assumed that since the Holy Spirit was opening my eyes to these issues, God must want me to minister to all of them. Right? No…Wrong! After a while it was so overwhelming that I would just try to shut these experiences off.

> I have learned that I am only responsible to minister as God directs.

Later I learned that I was not responsible to minister to every need that I perceived. I was only responsible to do what God specifically directed me to do. I learned to ask God how He wanted me to respond to what I saw. This sounds so simple, but it changed everything for me. If there were multiple issues to be ministered to, I asked God which one He wanted me to address.

In the counseling example described above, I learned that as someone was telling their story, I needed to ask God, "What is the one thing that you want me to address with this person today?" Then I followed the instructions from the Lord instead of thinking that I needed to solve a long history of problems.

As I apply that principle, I find that sometimes the Lord says, "I just want you to listen." Then I can relax and not even try to give input. In this way God takes His rightful place as Savior and Counselor and I am merely a mouthpiece. Asking God for direction takes off the pressure to perform.

> **REFLECTION**
> *Why is it important to seek God's direction about ministering to needs in other's lives?*

Finally, I enjoy going to parties again because I do not need to be responsible for all the needs that I sense. I only need to obey what God tells me to do. It really simplifies ministry life. I have learned that I am only responsible to minister as God directs, even when people are expecting or demanding something different.

DAY 5 — The Holy Spirit Presents God's Love

"For to one is given the word of wisdom through the Spirit, to another the word of knowledge through the same Spirit" (I Corinthians 12:8).

A while ago I attended a conference where Shawn Bolz was ministering. Shawn operates very accurately in the spiritual gift of words of knowledge. In the conference, he mentioned a prophetic word that he received several years before, indicating that God was going to use his life as an example for many. The word indicated that his experiences in words of knowledge and the prophetic would provide a bridge over which others would be able to walk in order to have similar experiences with God.

At the end of that conference, I received prayer for impartation. In the months that followed, I asked God to show me more specific words of knowledge for people when I was preaching. God had many times given me words of knowledge for healing, but I never received people's names, birthdates or facts about them.

Soon after, while speaking at a conference for DOVE churches in Toronto, Canada, I felt as if God showed me the name Ken and the word "orphans "during the worship time. Then, I saw a drop-down menu of names. The middle name, Jaclyn, stood out to me. As my speaking time was coming to an end I asked if there was a Ken or a Jaclyn present, and whether they had anything to do with orphans. No one responded. So I chalked it up as a learning experience.

The next morning, a Sunday, I was speaking at Harvest Church. After the service, the pastor was meeting with a first-time visitor, a lady. She introduced herself as Jackie. I asked if her birth name was Jaclyn and she said that it was. I asked her if she knew someone named Ken. She explained, "Ken is my father, but he recently passed away so I am just moving back to Toronto this weekend to be close to my other siblings because we are all feeling like orphans." I was so humbled as I explained to her that I had received part of these details the day before.

> God cares about and is involved in the emotional details of our lives.

I was so amazed at God. He loved Jaclyn so much that He gave me her name, her father's name and the word 'orphan' the day before—in a totally different meeting! Jaclyn was a mature adult, so I was not expecting her to describe the pain of losing her father in the words that she used: "we are all feeling like orphans." God cared about how she was feeling based on how she defined and experienced it.

If God cares that much for Jaclyn, then He also cares for each of us the same way. He cares about and is involved in the emotional details of our lives, especially when we experience loss or pain.

> **REFLECTION**
> *In what ways have you seen God's love communicated through the gifts of the Holy Spirit?*

There is a reason that the "Love Chapter" (1 Corinthians 13) is in between two chapters in the Bible that discuss the gifts of the Holy Spirit. It is because the Holy Spirit's gifts are the delivery service of God's love coming to people.

DAY 6: Words of Knowledge for Physical Healing

"On one of those days, as he was teaching, Pharisees and teachers of the law were sitting there, who had come from every village of Galilee and Judea and from Jerusalem. And the power of the Lord was with him to heal" (Luke 5:17).

I love that God sends His power to heal people! One of the ways that we recognize God's power is present with the intent to heal is through words of knowledge.

Before I am speaking somewhere I often take time to ask God specifically if there is any word of knowledge for healing that He would like me to highlight. I might feel a very slight pain or pressure on certain parts of my body that is not normal for me. After I write down where the pressure or pain is located, usually it goes away instantly.

At other times, a specific thought or picture flashes through my mind about a certain part of the human body. I understand this as God's direction. In both of these ways of receiving words of knowledge, the only way to test whether it was God or not is to simply ask if anyone has pain or a problem with that area. If people respond, I pray. If they do not respond, I still pray. It is a risk and step of faith to put yourself "out there" like this, but it is worth it.

One time I was ministering at a church for the first time in central Pennsylvania. Before the service I received a short list of body parts to call out and pray for specifically. At the time of ministry, I asked if anyone had certain pains and read through my list. One of the things on my list was a problem with compressed discs in someone's back; it was almost like the cartilage in the spine was compressed to the point of being non-existent. I do not have a medical background and did not know any specific medical terms for the condition I was trying to describe.

As I asked about this ailment, no one responded. But I asked again because I was feeling an intensity from the Lord about it. Again, no one responded. I asked several more times if someone had a close family or friend with that condition. No one came forward or indicated that they did. However, I noticed tears starting to run down the face of one lady. Still no one responded. I figured that if God wanted to touch someone, He could do it without me specifically laying hands on them. I prayed aloud that if anyone who was present had this particular problem, that the pain would go and that Jesus would touch and heal him or her. I then proceeded to minister on other topics.

Two years later the pastor of that church came to me at a leader's conference and told me there had been someone in the room that day who had that specific problem with her back. When I prayed out loud for it, she could feel God touching her but did not want to come forward. She was scheduled to have surgery on her discs within several days and did not want to testify without being sure that she was really healed. When she went to the doctor, it was confirmed that she had been healed. She did not need the surgery.

> I don't always know why some get healed and others do not. But I have determined to not let what does not happen stop what does happen!

It was two years until I heard that testimony of healing. This encourages me to continue to pray even if no one responds.

Many times I have seen God touch people and heal them to the point where they are able to do what they could not do before being prayed for. Not everyone about whom I had a word of knowledge has been healed, but many have, so I continue to pray. I don't always know why some get healed and others do not. But I have determined to not let what does not happen stop what does happen!

Once I was in a hurry to finish preaching at a church because the service needed to end by a certain time. Instead of asking people to respond to words of knowledge, I just prayed through the list of ailments that I felt I received from the Lord before the service. I did this to finish quickly and honor the time allotted. As I read through the list, I asked the audience to place their hands on the place that needed healing if it applied to them. I remember specifically praying for intense ear pain to be healed.

The next week one of the leaders told me that a lady in the service had very severe pain in her ear for a long time. She was on medication for that condition. As I called out that specific word of knowledge in prayer, the pain instantly left her ear and did not return. Praise Jesus. Isn't His healing power amazing?

REFLECTION
What can you do to see healings take place on a regular basis?

If you begin to receive the types of words of knowledge that I describe above, I encourage you to ask the people around you if that specific need is present. If you are in a church service or small group meeting, ensure that the leaders are comfortable with you doing this. Then pray, asking God to heal. Follow up that prayer by asking persons who were prayed for to test whether healing was taking place by trying to do something that they could not do before. Continue to pray until healing comes or the person does not want prayer any longer. Many times I have seen healing come on the second, third, or fourth time of praying. Sometimes the pain gets significantly less with each time of prayer.

DAY 7

Knowing the Mind of Christ

"Who may ascend into the hill of the Lord?
    Or who may stand in His holy place?
He who has clean hands and a pure heart,
    Who has not lifted up his soul to an idol,
    Nor sworn deceitfully" (Psalm 24:3-4).

The importance of keeping your soul free and clean cannot be overstated. Previously, we talked about our inner life with Christ. I would like to go a step further and discuss how we grow in hearing God's voice and understanding His will. In his book *God Secrets*,[1] Shawn Bolz talks about how our minds interact with God's mind.

In short, he discusses how the brain, undeveloped when we are born, is biologically wired to develop through interaction with other people. As we interact reciprocally with people close to us, our brains form similar synapses and patterns of thought. This also happens when we spend time interacting with God. Our minds also become more connected to the mind of Christ. The more time we spend with Him the more we become like Him and reflect His values. This is why sometimes His thoughts sound a lot like our thoughts, because we are thinking His thoughts!

One of the ways that God communicates with people is through what I call the screen of the imagination. This is the place where we experience dreams or internal visions. Consider the creative center of your brain as a movie projector. It projects from whatever source of inspiration it is connected to. If your inspiration is coming from God, you think a God-inspired thought. If there is no fear, doubt or negativity at work, that thought can freely become a picture (vision) in your mind. It can also become a lyric or melody, a sense of direction, an unfolding vision, a divine goal, or even a feeling of peace directly from God's heart.

If we allow our minds to become polluted with fear, negativity, conspiracy and impure thoughts, then the screen of our imagination becomes distorted. That is why it is important to guard the purity of our hearts and minds. We need to detach from the negative, sarcastic and caustic ways of worldly thought and consciously meditate on whatever is true, noble, just, pure, lovely, of good report, virtuous or praiseworthy as instructed in Philippians 4:8-9. In this place of pure thought, we receive words of wisdom, words of knowledge and prophetic revelation.

> It is important to guard the purity of our hearts and minds.

When my mind is free to be creative, I am able to hear God's thoughts more clearly. When my mind is burdened with fear, shame, intimidation or a negative outlook, I find it very difficult to receive God's thoughts. Though I do not claim to fully understand it, I know there is a direct link between the creative, unhindered free flow of thought and hearing God clearly.

A few days before I was scheduled to speak at a church, one of their missionaries who worked in a closed nation was killed. This young man was a husband and father and had been martyred. When I heard the news, knowing that I would need to share a relevant word, I sat for hours trying to get a message. Usually messages come as a download rather quickly for me, but not this time. To make matters more difficult, it happened in the same town that my brother and his entire family of four had tragically died in a plane crash ten years earlier. Though I did not personally know the young man who had been killed, I was acquainted with the grief of tragedy.

Fifteen minutes before I needed to leave for the service, I still did not have a message, even though I had been crying out for God to reveal to me what to share with this congregation that was in deep sorrow. It was only when I recognized that I had allowed the situation to intimidate me that I got a breakthrough. I realized that I was fearful, timid, and needed to repent. So I did. I repented for allowing myself to be intimidated by the fear of man. I realized that wondering so much about what people would think of my preaching in this very difficult circumstance had made me fearful and shut down my ability to hear God.

As soon as I repented, a very clear message dropped into my spirit. I immediately knew which Scriptures to use, where to start, and how to end the message that I was to share.

REFLECTION
Are there any impure thoughts, idols, or deceit you need to repent of so your heart and mind are free to engage with God's thoughts?

CHAPTER 7

Growing in a Supernatural Lifestyle

Merle Shenk

DAY 1 — Visions of Angels

"Are not the angels all ministering spirits (servants) sent out in the service [of God for the assistance] of those who are to inherit salvation?" (Hebrews 1:14, Amplified Bible).

Miracles do not happen by following formulas or prescribed prayers. Each situation is different, but the secret is being obedient to the nudging of the Holy Spirit.

Some years ago, God led me to act in an unusual way while praying. I was preaching at a church conference in the Kenyan town of Ngong, which is outside of Nairobi. During my stay, the pastor took me and another pastor on a long bus drive to a house in the country. The lady who lived there was extremely ill. As we were on the way, I sensed the Lord telling me that the lady had contracted HIV/Aids. I did not confirm this with the pastor before praying because I did not want my mind to be consumed with all the negative details related to this terrible illness. I wanted to focus on what I was sensing from the Lord.

> Miracles do not happen by following formulas or prescribed prayers.

When we arrived and after praying in tongues for only a few minutes, I received an internal vision of an angel standing about fifteen feet away in the corner of the room. As we were praying I ambled over to that corner and stood in the same way that I had seen the angel standing. Suddenly faith hit my spirit and I began to pray with a level of authority that surprised me. Immediately the woman vomited as she was delivered of a vile spirit. We continued to pray. Again, I saw an angel standing in front of her with his hand on her head and pointing at her stomach. Encouraged by the results of the previous experience, I again emulated the angel I saw in the screen of my mind. I walked in front of the lady, placed my hand on her head and pointed at her stomach. As I started to pray out loud a fearless authority overwhelmed me. The woman vomited again as we took authority over another symptom of the sickness that she was experiencing.

As we continued to pray and minister to the woman, I again saw in the screen of my mind an angel standing three feet behind the lady. The angel pointed at the lady's back. I walked over and stood behind the lady in the exact same position as I saw the angel and prayed emphatically. Again, the woman vomited. This time, we knew that she was completely delivered from Satan's grip.

The woman was very thankful. As we talked, I asked her cautiously if she was suffering from HIV/Aids. Because of the love and ministry that she had just experienced, we had gained her trust. She confirmed that she had been diagnosed with HIV/Aids, which she believed she had contracted through her husband who traveled far to work and stayed away for months at a time. We instructed the woman to go back to her doctors and continue to follow their instructions. I never told the other pastors or the lady what I had experienced while praying for her. This was so new to me; I just needed to meditate on it for a while. There are many secrets that can be held just between you and God.

> **REFLECTION**
> *Do you feel ready for God to use you in unexpected ways?*

On a subsequent ministry trip years later, I learned that the lady was healed that afternoon and was declared free of HIV/Aids by her doctors at her next medical exam.

In all my years of praying for others, this was the first time that I had an encounter like this with such a dramatic and immediate effect. The experience taught me to step out in faith with impressions and visions I have received and work with what God is showing me.

Fathered by God though a Stranger

DAY 2

"It is written in the Prophets, 'And they will all be taught by God.' Everyone who has heard and learned from the Father comes to me" (John 6:45).

At one point, God blessed my family with the ability to buy a property in another country along with a co-investor. I confess that I did not know a lot about the details of international investments; this was the start of a sharp learning curve. After several years I needed very specific advice about how to handle this property due to the changing dynamics in our personal lives.

While in that country, I had only one day to find all the answers to my specific questions. To make matters worse,

I was in a developing nation and I did not even know who to ask or even where to start! If you have ever tried to accomplish something in a developing nation that requires receiving and working with a lot of complicated information, you may understand how large of a mountain I was facing. I needed information on international banking, taxes, international investment and a few other things. I had about ten hours to accomplish it all. To say I was a bit stressed is an understatement. Confused about how to go about the task, I decided to start at the bank.

When I entered the bank, there were several long lines. This was not looking good! I did not know which line I was supposed to be in, so I jumped in a line that I thought seemed shortest. I began to pray... hard! I told God, "Lord, I need your help, I don't even know what questions to ask. I don't know whom I need to speak to. Please help me. I need you to 'father' me through somebody here. Show me the way."

Many of us have desired to have someone with experience who is able to mentor and coach us through challenges in life. I am no different. I had recently been reading John Eldridge's book *Fathered by God*[1] in which he explains how God can "father" you through random people in your life.

Soon a bank employee came down the line asking what people needed in order to ensure that everyone was in the correct line. When he reached me, I told him everything that I was looking for. He politely informed me that I was in the wrong line and that I needed to go to the long line instead.

As I walked up to the long line where people were seated on benches, a well dressed gentleman with a very large stack of papers entered the line in front of me. I made a light-hearted joke saying, "Oh no, I got stuck behind the man with a huge stack of papers!" We both laughed. Intrigued by my accent, we struck up a conversation. He asked me what I was doing in his country, and I told him about our ministry and recent changes and developments that were taking place.

> If we posture our hearts in a vulnerable and open position, God is able to use complete strangers to speak His wisdom to us!

At the risk of sounding really stupid, I decided to be as open as possible and tell him why I was at the bank. I told him that I was looking for advice on international investment, tax law, and international banking. He smiled and told me that he owned his own investment firm that specialized in international investments and tax law. He mentioned that he rarely comes to the bank himself, but usually gives that task to an employee. That day, however, it was necessary for him to come in person. I was stunned and amazed by God's goodness!

For the next forty-five minutes as we sat in that line, he systematically answered my questions. He told me what to ask when I reached the counter. He told me what I needed to do immediately and instructed me step by step on how to move forward with our property, including what to do with the tax laws. By the time we reached the counter, I was prepared. When I left, all my questions had been answered and I had a strategy in place! I walked out of the bank after two hours, completely shocked by what had just happened. God had fathered me through that man. He did not even know it, but God was using him to mentor me. He gave me almost an hour of his time while we sat in the line, the time for which he would have charged most people several hundred dollars.

In this experience, I learned the value of being open with your life. I am normally a private individual, especially when it comes to finances. But because I openly shared what I needed, God could use this man to speak into my life. There have been other times when I was open, but felt scorned by people as a result. Yet in retrospect, I realize that I could have sat in that line for almost an hour, making small talk and being worried about what I was going to do. I would have totally missed an encounter that God had for me.

REFLECTION
What types of things can hinder us from experiencing divine encounters?

Just like God owns the cattle on a thousand hills and He uses them to sustain us, He also holds all the knowledge that you and I need for challenging situations in our lives. There is always a solution in His mind. If we posture our hearts in a vulnerable and open position, God is able to use complete strangers to speak His wisdom to us!

DAY 3

God's Touch through Others

"No one has seen God at any time. The only begotten Son, who is in the bosom of the Father, He has declared Him" (John 1:18).

Jesus dwells in the bosom of the Father. This is where He is positioned in God.

I once had an encounter with the Father's love through Dave Hess, a pastor in south central Pennsylvania. Dave's story in itself is incredible as he survived a near-death encounter with leukemia and appendicitis at the same time. He shares this miraculous testimony in his book *Hope Beyond Reason*.[2]

I invited Dave to minister on the topic of the Father's love at one of the schools of supernatural ministry I was directing. As he unfolded truths about the Father's love from the Word of God, he included this Scripture from John 1:18. He described that the *bosom* of the Father literally means "between the shoulder blades." Taken literally, this is right next to His heart.

Dave then gave a visible illustration that shows what this looks like. He asked me to come forward, wrapped me in a big bear hug and held me for several minutes as he continued talking about how Jesus dwells in the embrace of the Father. As he ministered, I had an encounter with the Father's love in a way that I never had before.

At the time I was not particularly a "touchy-feely" kind of guy. The only affection that I shared at all was with those closest to me in my immediate family. I did not like public displays of affection towards me. In that embrace, God ministered something to me about the value of His embrace. I was ministered to in a very deep way. I received an impartation of the Father's love, passed on to me through Dave.

> Take some time to sit and let the Father's love embrace your heart.

I went back to our church and began to minister on the Father's love. In our church it was normal for us to have times of ministry and prayer. For months after this encounter, I would feel directed by God to hug people in the same way and pray and minister to them as I held them. Even though it was God's leading, I found it to be incredibly awkward and uncomfortable, especially when I had to ask people that I did not even know if I could give them a hug and pray for them. Time and time again, people would break down in huge sobs as I prayed. God was ministering the love of the Father through me. People were hearing that they were not forgotten, they were not alone and they were not unloved. Many deep father wounds were healed over this time.

I have grown more accustomed to giving godly affection to people in times of ministry. The benefits of seeing people ministered to far outweigh my own awkwardness. If I need to be uncomfortable in order for people to receive from God, then so be it! After all, touch is a "love language" that

God has created. Many in the church are deeply hungry for our Father's love.

In John 14:3 Jesus says, "And if I go and prepare a place for you, I will come again and receive you to Myself; that where I am, there you may be also."

Jesus did not say "that where I *will be*...." He said "that where I *am*." That is present tense. It is happening currently. In other words, the place that Jesus prepared for us is the same place in the Father's embrace where He continually dwells! Yes, there will come a time when Jesus will return and we will be with Him. However, this love of the Father is available to us today in real time, in our present place and situation.

REFLECTION
Why is it important for us to receive the affection of God's heart?

Take some time to sit and let the Father's love embrace your heart. If possible, use the opportunity to get some bread and wine or grape juice and celebrate the Lord's supper with Him.

The Joy of Healing

DAY 4

"Then one of the synagogue rulers, named Jairus, came there. Seeing Jesus, he fell at his feet and implored him earnestly, saying, 'My little daughter is at the point of death. Come and lay your hands on her, so that she may be made well and live'" (Mark 5:22-23).

A young lady who was Muslim had just received Jesus as her Lord and Savior the week before her daughter was hospitalized with a very serious blood infection. I was called to pray for the little girl who had been put into an induced coma so that she would not pull out the tubes that were inserted into her throat and under her chest cavity. While I was there, the girl's father and his family started to gather around. He and his family were still Muslim.

The doctors instructed the mother to call all her daughter's loved ones to say goodbye, because there was nothing else that could be done for her medically. Her condition was deteriorating fast. Understandably, the mood around the bed was very somber. The young mother who had recently given her life to Jesus and was new to Christianity must have heard about anointing oil because there was a bottle of extra virgin olive oil sitting beside the bed and the little girl's hair was wet with oil. She spent day after day praying for her daughter and laying hands on her. Now because of what the doctor had told her, she called for me and Valerie, one of the church elders, to come and pray and dedicate her daughter to the Lord.

Standing beside the bed, we began to pray and lay hands on the little girl. We prayed

> As we prayed, I knew in my heart that this little girl was not going to die but would live.

with the family standing around us. Suddenly, it was as if a shaft of joy hit my heart and began to bubble over! I was embarrassed because it was everything that I could do to keep from being visibly giddy and laughing out loud! I thought, "Oh, Lord, help me stay composed." I could not hide the smile on my face as I prayed. In my heart I knew that this little girl was not going to die but would live. As we finished, I encouraged the mom to continue to stand in faith for her daughter. I felt it was not yet the end for this little girl.

I left to go to another appointment and Valerie stayed behind. Later she called me and said, "Pastor, you should have seen what happened." She narrated how the father's family wanted to bring in some spiritualists to 'pray,' but her mother (a week old in her faith) stood over that girl like a 'momma bear,' hands planted on either side of her daughter saying, "you will not touch my daughter; we are Christians now!"

> **REFLECTION**
> *What are some promises of God that you are standing for?*

Her daughter's recovery started that very day. After several weeks of growing stronger and stronger, she was released from the hospital. It was such a joy to later see her, joyful and vibrant, running around at our church. She is a testimony of God's goodness and healing power poured out for a brave and courageous young mother. The doctors call her their miracle child. She was at the door of death, but Jesus brought her back. Praise the Lord!

Ephesians 6:13-14 says that when we have reached the end of all that we know to do with the Word of God, we are to stand firm. That is exactly what this young mother did.

Encounters that bring Healing

"He listened to Paul speaking. And Paul, looking intently at him and seeing that he had faith to be made well, said in a loud voice, 'Stand upright on your feet.' And he sprang up and began walking" (Acts 14:9-10).

The week before we were to begin one of the Schools of Supernatural Ministry that I led, we held prayer meetings with some of our staff. We were using a 24/7 house of prayer that was open to the public, so other people were free to come in and out during the time we were praying.

At the end of our time we prayed for each person who was present. As we prayed for one elderly gentleman who had joined us, we began to give him words of encouragement from the Lord. When I asked if he had need for physical healing, he asked for prayer for his feet. He explained that he loved to run and at a younger age he had been a semi-pro basketball player. Because of crippling pain in his feet, he could now only walk very slowly. This pain was growing markedly worse over the last ten to fifteen years and was now making it very difficult for him to get around. We prayed for his feet and commanded any spirit of infirmity to leave his body, and gave him several prophetic words.

Later that day he called the office to say that his feet were completely pain free! God healed him. When he felt the healing manifest, he went immediately to the gym. He had just finished a mile when he called us! Praise the Lord.

When we are available to pray for others with authority, God moves through us to touch people's lives. When we are faithful to move in the measure of faith that we have, God can do mighty things! Infirmities that have bound people for decades can be healed and lifted from someone's life in a moment!

> Make every encounter with people an opportunity for God to move.

Be encouraged to make every encounter with people an opportunity for God to move. Many times when we have guests in our home, we end our time together with prayer and the receiving and giving of prophetic words and impressions. This is something that we would do on a regular basis when on the mission field. Great life and encouragement come from this constant environment of prayer and hearing God's words for each other.

The atmosphere of a house of prayer helps create a healthy expectation for God to move in supernatural ways. We can create an atmosphere of God's presence around us in our lives through our relationship with Him!

Cultivate an atmosphere of prayer and expectation for God to move in the everyday moments of your life. When we are obedient, He does not disappoint us.

REFLECTION
What can you do to create an atmosphere of expectation of miracles in your home?

Miracles of Provision

DAY 6

"Each one must give as he has decided in his heart, not reluctantly or under compulsion, for God loves a cheerful giver. And God is able to make all grace abound to you, so that having all sufficiency in all things at all times, you may abound in every good work" (2 Corinthians 9:7-8, ESV).

My wife and I always strive to be generous with our finances. We tithe faithfully and give as much as we can beyond that amount. Many times, we have sensed God instructing us to give even more than what we thought we could afford. We discussed the instructions, prayed in faith and gave as we felt led.

In our formative years in ministry we heard a teaching from 2 Samuel 24:24, a time when Araunah wanted to give King David the threshing floor, oxen, and wood to offer as a burnt offering to the Lord. David responded, "No, but I will buy it from you for a price. I will not offer burnt offerings to the Lord my God that cost me nothing."

We have also seen great miracles of provision. God has set up divine timing for getting jobs and in later years, investment opportunities. In most cases we did not know how good some of these moves were financially until after we walked into them. The breakthroughs were definitely not due to our investing prowess!

In the early years of our ministry, there were many times when we did not have enough money to make it through the end of the month. Cheree and I were in agreement that we believed God would want us to always fulfill our financial obligations. If He did not provide in some way and needs could not be met, we would need to leave the mission field and move back home.

One incident took place when we were in Bible school. Our rent was due and we did not have the full amount to pay. When we went to the landlords to tell them that we could not pay, they told us that someone from our church had stopped by to pay our rent earlier that day. We were so shocked! We had not told anyone about our financial situation! But God moved upon someone's heart to bless us on the very day that we were out of money!

> Trusting God is not always easy, but it is always worth it.

Another time while serving in South Africa, our health insurance, rent, credit card payment and some other bills were all due in one week. The total amount that we owed was several thousand dollars! We had fifty dollars to our name! We were stressed, to say the least. In fact, we told each other that we probably reached the end of our time on the mission field. "I guess we need to leave this outreach and go home," I concluded.

I drove to an Internet café to check our bank balance in the USA so that I could plot the way forward. Guess what! Someone had given us a $3,000 financial gift that was deposited the day before! Praise God. This person did not know—actually no one else apart from God and us knew—how close we were to giving up!

Another time I paid an airline ticket for a ministry trip with air miles points. In the months leading up to that trip, our finances became very tight. I remember the distress of having thirty dollars to our name, and leaving my wife and young children in order to go to an interior African country for ministry. I would have cancelled the trip, but because I had booked my ticket with air miles, it could not be refunded.

The day before I left, my wife packed a large jar of peanut butter in my suitcase. She was thinking that I would be able to survive on that peanut butter the entire two-and-a-half weeks and therefore not starve. That night a dear friend of ours was shopping and felt as if God told him to buy our family a half of a lamb. He was not sure why… he thought there may be symbolism involved since Jesus was the Lamb of God. But we knew why! This meat was going to last my family for the entire time I was out of the country!

As I packed my clothes, I decided to take along several batches of teaching CD's that I had recorded. I was traveling African style, which means I was not staying in hotels but rather staying in people's homes and being hosted by churches that had invited me to come to preach. On that trip, the CD's sold out. I had to make twice as many again while in the host country, and those all sold too! I was able to use that money to pay for transportation, bless each host home that I stayed in and pay for all my needs! When I returned home I handed the unopened peanut butter jar back to my wife with a big smile on my face! God had provided!

The Word of God promises us, "And my God will supply every need of yours according to his riches in glory in Christ Jesus" (Philippians 4:19).

We had a significant experience at a conference when, during worship, people started coming spontaneously—without anyone making an appeal—to lay offerings on the altar. People gave and gave. Some laid shoes, jackets, or money at the altar. Another gave a set of car keys. I remember a little girl probably around six years old, coming forward to lay a very well-loved stuffed animal on the altar. It was a holy moment.

At this time, Cheree felt the desire to give her diamond ring. She felt that it was an ultimate act of surrender and worship, laying her most precious possession down as an offering to the Lord. She asked me if it was okay and I consented, saying that if God was asking for that level of sacrifice, I would support her.

Now, several years later, I was looking for a gift for our anniversary, and I felt as if the Lord instructed me to buy Cheree a nice ring with several diamonds. Overwhelmed by the price tag, I was uncertain if I should spend what was for us in that season of our lives a very high price! I confess that this was the only time that I had ever felt God tell me to buy something on a credit card that I was not sure that I had the money to pay for. I even preach against this practice, but I felt certain that it was God who was directing me, and took the step of obedience.

A day or two later I was contacted by someone who was selling a high value asset. She explained that she and her husband had decided to give part of the proceeds to us, but that they were having trouble selling it. No one had expressed interest in buying this asset for several weeks.

> **REFLECTION**
> *In what ways have you experienced unexpected provision in your life?*

Within twenty-four hours from the time we talked, they made a sale. The amount of money given to us was almost the exact cost of the ring. God provided funds to replace the ring Cheree had sacrificially given away several years before with one that is much nicer.

Trusting God is not always easy, but it is always worth it.

Catalyst Relationships

"And let us consider how to stir up one another to love and good works (Hebrews 10:24).

Several friends have encouraged me greatly in ministering in the supernatural. Together, we have seen God do incredible things. Joa from the Netherlands is one such friend. We worked together on the mission field and did things together that neither of us would have found ourselves doing on our own.

One time, by coincidence, we met an old friend in a shopping mall and we started to pray for him. By the time we were finished we were prophesying uninhibitedly (and loudly) over his life and also praying for others. It was obvious that when we were together, we would step out in faith more than when we were alone. There was a mutual encouragement that we would both experience when working together. We would lead church meetings in dangerous parts of squatter camps late at night. We would pray for the sick and see God ministering healing to people's bodies. We would prophesy over people for hours!

Another close friend, Nigel, and I often experience the same type of encouragement from working with each other. Often we stopped to get gas and ended up praying for the attendant at the gas station. We would visit people's homes and then pray and prophesy over people as God would stir us. We would pray for people who were living on the street for emotional needs and physical healing, then also provided them with meals and helped them find shelter. We have often seen acute pain leaving peoples' bodies miraculously due to these prayers.

In a home in Kenya, where we had traveled together, God used us to minister to an 80-year-old man who was 100 percent deaf in one ear and 50 percent deaf in the other. Nigel says, "I knew that Merle was going to want pray for healing for this man, and I didn't have the faith to even start." And it is true. I started to pray for healing—but it was

Nigel who was bold enough in faith to snap his fingers to test the man's hearing. I honestly didn't feel brave enough to do this! But somewhere between me initiating the prayer and Nigel stepping out to boldly test his hearing, this man's hearing began to return. Encouraged by one another, we prayed more, and his hearing was completely restored. After prayer, we shared the Gospel and the elderly man gave his life to Jesus. The whole process took about forty minutes. If I had been alone I probably would have just prayed briefly and moved on.

Working together with empowering relationships can be a catalyst to help push us beyond the normal comfort level in our lives. Working together encourages us to push through in extended prayer times to see miracles happen. I have recognized this dynamic with other people through various seasons in my life. Another such relationship is with Kevin Kazemi, one of the co-authors of this book. I highly value these relationships in my life, because together we can accomplish more in God!

> Working together with empowering relationships can help push us beyond the normal comfort level in our lives.

When reading Acts 16:25, I have often wondered whether, if Paul and Silas had not been chained together in the same prison that night, they would still have prayed loudly and sang praises? Would they have experienced the same deliverance?

Jesus sent disciples out in groups of two for a reason. I believe that when we find people who stir us in faith, and encourage us to do greater things in God, we need to pay attention. We should value these relationships and do whatever we can to function together in them. And the converse is also true: we should also avoid relationships that drain our faith or discourage us from doing works of faith.

REFLECTION
Why do you think Jesus sent people out in teams of two or more to minister?

CHAPTER 8

You Too can Encounter the Supernatural!

Larry Kreider

Angelic Protection

DAY 1

As you read through the chapters in this book, you read many stories of the supernatural spirit world that includes both angels and demons. Angels, according to the Scriptures, provide supernatural protection to those of us who are following Christ. "Are they not all ministering spirits sent forth to minister for those who will inherit salvation?" (Hebrews 1:14).

A few years ago I met a Christian businessman in Malaysia, who told his story of being kidnapped for ransom. The kidnapper opened the car door and forced the businessman out of the driver's seat into the passenger's seat. Another kidnapper jumped into the back seat and at gunpoint forced the businessman to hold his hands behind his back. After driving a distance, the kidnappers needed to come to a stop when they got into a heavy traffic jam. When the businessman looked outside the car, he saw an angel open the car door. The kidnappers were so terrified by the sight of the angel that they quickly turned into a side street and ran into a street light pole bringing the car to a screeching halt. Two police officers were standing there and took the two kidnappers into custody. The businessman gives all the credit to the Lord for sending the angel. Our God sends angels to protect His people!

With today's terrorists attacking innocent people at airports and other public places, we must trust God for supernatural protection. The Scriptures teach us: "For he will command his angels concerning you to guard you in all your ways" (Psalm 91:11). Praise God for angels serving behind the scenes who battle for those who are committed to Jesus Christ!

One evening at dusk a couple from our church family stopped at an ATM machine to withdraw money.

> Our God sends angels to protect His people!

They were having trouble with pushing the right keys, so both got out of the car to stand in front of the ATM machine to read the instructions better. The bank was closed and no one else was around. Suddenly a car careened into the drive-through behind them and came to a screeching halt. Five tough guys jumped out of the car and surrounded them. Terrified, the wife, cried, "Jesus, help." She glanced toward the glass bank door. Although it did not open, a man about 7-feet tall appeared on the other side. The wife waved at the figure inside. The guys looked in the direction where she was waving, then jumped back into their car and tore off. The figure behind the door also disappeared.

You may not always be aware of the presence of angels around you. Neither can you predict how they will appear, but God has angels all around us to protect us!

This explains the verse in the Bible that says, "Do not forget to entertain strangers, for by so doing some people have entertained angels without knowing it" (Hebrews 13:2). Just because you have never seen an angel does not mean angels are not present with you.

My wife, LaVerne, is convinced that I have many angels who protect me while I drive, because I often get so preoccupied while driving that I need supernatural intervention to keep the car on the road!

Although angels are spirits, they make themselves visible when needed. While vacationing in Mexico, family friends took an early morning stroll along the beach. Gorgeous weather and the clear waters enticed them to go for a swim. When they tried to return to shore, the undercurrent was so strong, they could not swim back. (Later they noticed that black flags were posted to warn of dangerous undercurrents.) Calling on the name of Jesus and battling the waves, they eventually made it back to shore, but the husband collapsed and did not respond to any nudging and pleas to answer questions. His skin turned eerie shades before becoming a deathly blue. He looked as if he were dying. Because they had wandered much farther from civilization than they realized, no one else was on the beach.

As this man's wife was pleading for Jesus to help, a black man, who looked to be at least seven feet tall, appeared. He took one glance at my friend and said, "I know exactly what is wrong. His lungs are filled with water." He pushed and pressed against his back until water gushed from his mouth. Then the stranger said, "He'll be fine. Just let him rest. Don't worry." The man disappeared as quickly as he had come. Two hours later, my friend finally had enough strength to sit up. Although weak, he was fine. Was that coincidence? Was it a man jogging on the secluded beach, or an angel?

There have been angelic sightings all over the world. I have a close relative who saw an angel in her bedroom during a time of great need for comfort and hope. She recalls that deep peace came over her when she had the angelic visitation.

REFLECTION
How do we know we have angels protecting us?

A friend of mine was detained in Albania many years ago for handing out Bibles. Miraculously she and her friend were released. The only problem was that they were released in the middle of nowhere, each with a heavy suitcase. It was miles to the Yugoslavian border. A man stopped and offered to drive them through the countryside and straight to the border. After he dropped them off, he simply disappeared. They were convinced it was an angel who had provided help in their time of need.

Let's thank God for angels, ministering spirits, sent forth to minister for each of us who are inheriting salvation. Pray for our eyes to be opened to God's supernatural protection.

Weapons of Warfare

Learning to live in the supernatural includes understanding three powerful spiritual weapons the Lord gives to us to defeat the spirits of darkness.

The first weapon is the name of Jesus Christ. The scriptures tell us, "That at the name of Jesus every knee should bow, in heaven and on earth and under the earth, and every tongue confess that Jesus Christ is Lord, to the glory of God the Father" (Philippians 2:10-11).

Some time ago, I was awakened in the night and sensed an evil presence in my room. I was away from home, and no one else was in the house where I was staying. I felt as if I was frozen to my bed. I could only call out the name of "Jesus." Again and again I spoke the name of Jesus, Jesus, Jesus. The evil presence left and I was able to go back to sleep. There is power in the name of Jesus.

> God has given us three powerful spiritual weapons to defeat the spirits of darkness.

The second weapon the Lord has given to us against the enemy is the blood of Jesus Christ. I have personally witnessed demons in people who have shrieked in fear at the mention of the blood of Jesus. On one occasion, a man with demons held his hands over his ears and screamed when the blood of Jesus was mentioned. The blood of the Lamb has freed us from the power of the enemy. The Scriptures tell us in Revelation 12:11, "They overcame him by the blood of the Lamb and by the word of their testimony; they did not love their lives so much as to shrink from death."

The third weapon the Lord has given to us against the enemy is the word of our testimony. Our testimony is simply confessing what the Lord has done in our lives and what God is saying about us. We know what God says about us by believing His Word. The truth of God's Word sets us free.

"Therefore submit to God. Resist the devil and he will flee from you. Draw near to God and He will draw near to you" (James 4:7, 8).

Smith Wigglesworth was an evangelist in Great Britain years ago. He compared the devil to a stray dog that is barking at our heels. The evangelist taught that unless we resist the dog, he will continue with his "yelping" and aggravation. But if we boldly tell him to leave us alone, he will flee. The devil has no choice when we resist him in Jesus' name. He must flee.

> **REFLECTION**
> *What are the three weapons the Lord gives to us so we can defeat the spirits of darkness?*

A Supernatural Gift of Faith

An acquaintance of mine tells the story of a man who was coming home late one night to his apartment in New York City. Suddenly a robber jumped out of the dark and told him to give him all of his money. With a gun pointed at him, the only thing that came to the man's mind was to trust God. God gave him an instant message of knowledge, and he told the thief that his mother (the thief's mother) was praying for his salvation and constantly talked with him about his need for the Lord.

The robber was stunned and frightened and said, "How did you know those things? I'm out of here! This is too crazy!" With that the robber did indeed leave.

This man was spared from being robbed and possibly harmed because he not only believed that the supernatural spiritual gifts are for all believers, but he also made use of them. He had supernaturally received from the Lord a "gift of faith" and a "message of knowledge" and encountered the supernatural.

A "gift of faith" is the extraordinary confidence that God gives and unwavering belief in God's ability to fulfill His purposes. The gift of faith is not our theology. It is not the same as saving faith (Ephesians 2:8) nor is it our confidence or hope that something will happen. It is not faith confessions, ordinary faith (2 Corinthians 5:7) or the prayer of faith. The spiritual gift of faith is a supernatural manifestation of the Spirit of God who miraculously drops the assurance of the answer into our hearts before we see it happen with our natural eyes. It is believing that we have it when we pray (Mark 11:24). It ceases to be faith the minute we see it come to pass.

> When the gift of faith operates, it changes everything.

The gift of faith caused Abraham to claim that God had given him a son even before he saw any evidence. Abraham understood that God "calls things that are not as though they were" (Romans 4:17). Stephen, full of faith, was enabled to perform miracles (Acts 6:8).

A person with the gift of faith acts in complete confidence of God's ability to overcome obstacles. A gift of faith causes us to ask God for what is needed and trust the Lord for His provision. Often, the gift of faith and gifts of healing are strongly connected.

When the gift of faith operates, it changes everything. This faith does not come by study. It is not the faith that is a normal part of every Christian. For example, there is a natural faith we have that tells us that when we plant a seed it will produce a crop. Or if we go fishing in the right spot, we will catch fish. In fact, even non-Christians have this kind of faith.

The gift of faith is different from other types of faith. This is the kind of faith that allowed Moses to part the Red Sea. This kind of faith makes us immovable and unshakeable. When we are operating in the gift of faith we are experiencing the faith of God. Sometimes a gift of faith and a gift of supernatural knowledge or wisdom go hand in hand (1 Corinthians 12:8).

REFLECTION
Have you ever experienced a gift of faith?

A message of knowledge is supernaturally imparted by the Holy Spirit and is only a portion of God's total knowledge. This "power to know something we do not know in the natural" does not give us all knowledge, but rather is a specific word of knowledge given by the Holy Spirit. It is a portion of God's endless storehouse of knowledge. It can come as a thought, impression on our mind, or a vision. A gift of wisdom gives us the supernatural ability to properly use the knowledge we receive from God.

Let's take steps in faith today and trust God for these supernatural manifestations in our lives.

DAY 4

Testing Supernatural Manifestations

When God speaks to us prophetically or through another supernatural gift, it has the power to release new faith and expectation in our hearts. Sometimes a single word from God can change the atmosphere. We move from fear to overcoming faith. What seemed so helpless and hopeless suddenly becomes possible. God may not tell you your whole life's plan, but He will give you the courage and faith to take the next step. However, according to the Scriptures, supernatural prophecies and gifts need to be tested.

"Do not stifle the Holy Spirit. Do not scoff at prophecies, but test everything that is said. Hold on to what is good" (1 Thessalonians 5:19-21). Testing a prophecy may mean going to our pastor or another trusted Christian leader to present the prophecy to them and ask for their input. Additionally, all prophecy must be tested by the Scriptures. If something does not line up with the Bible, do not receive it.

Bible teacher Derek Prince once said that not testing a prophecy is "like turning a young person loose in a very fast sports car without checking the steering and the brakes. He may end up in a wreck. Over the years, I have seen scores and scores of wrecks through the misuse of prophecy. I have seen homes broken up, churches divided, and people ruined financially and in other ways through the wrong use of prophecy. Prophecy is an extremely powerful instrument, and if it is misused, it can be misused to the destruction of people."[1]

We must especially test a prophetic word for its meaning and timing. It may be for today or it may be for ten years in the future. We must be careful not to assume we know how and when to act upon a personal prophecy. I learned this the hard way. Several years ago I had two prophetic messages spoken over me about being called to minister to young people just as I had more than two decades before. One prophetic message came from a pastor in Oregon and the other came from a Presbyterian pastor in New Zealand. I assumed from receiving these two nearly identical prophecies that I was to start a youth ministry, so I did. I began meeting with about thirty-five youth every week in my hometown.

> Operating in any spiritual gift takes practice.

Shortly thereafter, the Lord brought me into a relationship with some young leaders who had started a weekly Bible study called "Tuesday Bible Study" (TBS). As our friendship grew, these leaders started to look to me as one of their spiritual advisors for their fledgling group. While the youth ministry I had started was declining (because it really wasn't in God's timing and I missed God's meaning) the TBS youth ministry was growing to one thousand young people!

I finally realized that I missed the timing of God. He did not want me to immediately start a new youth ministry. He called me to be a mentor to these young leaders. If I had waited to see what God was going to do with TBS, I wouldn't have started the other youth ministry. Timing is always a critical part of seeing a prophetic word come to pass. Getting the wrong timing for prophetic words is the most common error people make in processing prophecy.

If somebody tells you through a prophecy to go to the mission field, please don't quit your job unless you know that God has also spoken this same word to you and it is confirmed in other ways. The Lord speaks through His peace, circumstances and His still, small voice. I've seen people get into horrible problems by trying to run their lives based on what other people told them was a "prophetic message from God."

If the prophecy you receive doesn't bear agreement in your heart, you often will know it by a lack of peace in your spirit. Something tells you things are not quite right.

A lot of well-meaning people think they are hearing from God for others but the truth is they are not. If someone prophesies something to you that is not already in your heart, I suggest you write down the words that are spoken over you and wait for the Lord to reveal to you whether or not the words are from Him. If it is from God, He will clearly show you.

Operating in any spiritual gift takes practice. Not many people will begin by prophesying perfectly. Paul said those with the gift of prophecy should "prophesy in proportion to their faith" (Romans 12:6). As we begin to prophesy, we will grow and mature in the use of this supernatural gift.

When I feel an impression to give a prophetic message, I often ask myself these three questions: "Lord, is this from you?" "Lord, is this something you have given to me to share with others, or is it just for me to pray more effectively?" "Lord, is this for now, or for later?"

At times I have felt the Lord give me a prophetic message in a meeting, but also sense that I should wait to share it. Later, someone else gives the same message either through a prophecy or testimony or through a message from scripture. These incidents affirm that I have heard from God.

When I give an individual a prophetic message, I usually say something like: "I sense the Lord may be saying..." rather than "thus says the Lord." We often turn people off by our super-spiritual mannerisms, our traditions, or by our personalities. I sometimes encounter older ministers who prophesy in King James English. It is unclear to me why someone getting a word from God would chose to speak like they did during the King James era. Even so, it is best to look beyond the language used and the vessel God has chosen in order to concentrate on the word of the Lord.

REFLECTION
Have you ever received a prophecy that was life-changing for you?

You could say that a prophecy is like a clear, clean refreshing stream of water from the Lord. However, the channel or person who gives the prophetic message is like a hose. So we should not be surprised when the prophecy tastes a bit like the hose! We must discern between the message from the Lord and the hose—the person giving the message.

Praying in Tongues Bypasses the devil

I have been praying in tongues for more than forty years. Many times I have made the assumption that nearly everyone prays in tongues, but then I am reminded that this is not true. Speaking in tongues has helped me to encounter the supernatural. I want to take a moment to explain from Scripture how and why we speak in tongues for those who may be reading this book and have not spoken in tongues.

According to the Scriptures, we can pray two ways—with our mind and with our spirit. Both are needed, and both are under the influence of the Holy Spirit, according to 1 Corinthians 14:14-15. "For if I pray in tongues, my spirit is praying, but I don't understand what I am saying. Well then, what shall I do? I will pray in the spirit, and I will also pray in words I understand. I will sing in the spirit, and I will also sing in words I understand."

The first way we pray is with our mind. When we pray, "Our Father in heaven..." it is coming from our mind. We understand it. We are using our intellect to pray in a learned language. The second way we pray is with our spirit. When we pray with our spirit (in tongues), it's unfruitful to our mind. Our spirit is praying directly to the Father without having to accept the limitations of our human intellect.

In other words, when you and I pray with our spirit, we have no idea what we are saying but our heavenly Father knows what we are saying. We come in simple faith and trust God to provide the form of the words and their meaning to Him. Using our new language, we edify ourselves or "build ourselves up" spiritually (1 Corinthians 14:4). It is like a direct phone line to God. I pray in tongues daily, because when I pray in my spiritual language, I bypass the devil. He has no idea what I am saying. I am speaking the "language of angels" and "mysteries" according to the Bible (1 Corinthians 13:1; 14:2).

How important is it for us as Christians to speak in spiritual languages? Paul the apostle wished that every person spoke in tongues and stressed that the gift of tongues was an important part of his spiritual life. "I wish you could all speak in tongues...I thank God that I speak in tongues more than any of you" (1 Corinthians 14:5; 14:18).

> We can pray two ways: with our mind and with our spirit.

Is someone a second-rate Christian if they don't speak in a spiritual language? No, but God wants us to be blessed and use these blessings so we can fulfill His call on our lives. Some say they believe it is selfish to pray in tongues. Is it selfish to pray in English? Is it selfish to read the Bible? Why do we pray and read the Scriptures and speak in spiritual languages? We do it to communicate with God and encounter the supernatural as we are built up spiritually so that we can be effective in helping other people.

Tongues are an underrated gift. It is easy to make light of something we may not understand. There are different uses for this powerful gift. The most important aspect of tongues is for our own personal devotional life. We can speak in tongues in our prayer language with which we edify ourselves (1 Corinthians 14:4a). Paul did not diminish this important gift saying, "I thank God that I speak in tongues more than any of you" (1 Corinthians 14:18). He expressed how tongues were extremely useful in his prayer life. Jude tells us that when we pray in the Spirit, or in tongues, that we are actually building ourselves up in the holy faith (Jude 1:20).

A friend told me about a man who was vacationing in the mountains. On his way back to the southern part Florida, while driving at night, he felt the need to pray. He did not know what the need was so he just prayed in tongues. As he drove down the Florida Turnpike late that night, a car approached from the rear. As it passed he heard a loud noise and something hit his car. He stopped at the next service plaza to look at his car but did not notice anything unusual. The next day, however, he could see that a bullet had hit the little strip of metal that held the windshield in place. That strip of metal saved his life when someone shot at his car the night before. Around the same time, several other people were killed in this fashion on the turnpike.

God protected him. He was convinced that his time of praying in tongues provided supernatural protection for him and his wife.

The Scriptures talk of different kinds of tongues. There are different uses for tongues. My friend Dennis DeGrasse explains, "I have experienced this in my own life. I remember several times in which the Holy Spirit opened my mouth to talk to people in other languages. One in particular stands out. A Hispanic brother in a church in Florida spoke English with no problem, but as I began to prophesy over him I heard myself speaking in tongues. Spanish began to pour out of my mouth. He was very excited about the word and said, 'If that comes to pass I will be a wealthy man.' I inquired what the word was about and he told me it was about cattle. He was a cowboy, which I did not know. Several years later I saw him again. He affirmed that the prophetic word had indeed come to pass."[2]

REFLECTION
What are some of the different types of tongues we read about in the Bible?

Some may argue that these gifts passed away with the Apostle John, but that stance is completely unbiblical. The Bible says that tongues will cease when "perfection comes" (1 Corinthians 13:10). Some people believe that verse means tongues are no longer needed today. They believe that "perfection" refers to the Bible. They fail to realize that the same passage says we shall see "face to face." We will not see the Bible face to face. We will see Jesus face to face. At that time, at the end of the age, there will be no need for the gift of tongues. But until we see Jesus face to face, the Lord has given us the gifts of tongues, prophecy and other supernatural gifts of the Holy Spirit to use for His glory here on earth.

Do not try to interpret the Bible through your experiences, the opinions of others or through what makes sense to you. Let the Bible speak for itself and believe what it says. It is simple, direct and written so that the common man can understand it.

If you have never been baptized in the Holy Spirit or spoken in tongues, ask the Lord to fill you with His Spirit. He is faithful. Jesus says he gives the Holy Spirit to those who ask Him (Luke 11:13).

Supernatural Divine Appointments

Luke chapter nineteen tells us what happened when Jesus entered Jericho and made His way through the town. A man named Zacchaeus, who was the chief tax collector in the region, had become very rich. He tried to get a look at Jesus, but he was too short to see over the crowd. So he ran ahead and climbed a sycamore-fig tree beside the road, for Jesus was going to pass that way.

When Jesus came by, he looked up at Zacchaeus and called him by name. "Zacchaeus!" he said. "Quick, come down! I must be a guest in your home today." Zacchaeus quickly climbed down and took Jesus to his house in great excitement and joy, but the people were displeased. "He has gone to be the guest of a notorious sinner," they grumbled.

Meanwhile, Zacchaeus stood before the Lord and said, "I will give half my wealth to the poor, Lord, and if I have cheated people on their taxes, I will give them back four times as much!" Jesus responded, "Salvation has come to this home today, for this man has shown himself to be a true son of Abraham. For the Son of Man came to seek and save those who are lost" (Luke 19:1-10).

> The Lord loves to give us divine appointments, connecting us with the right people at the right time.

Zacchaeus had a divine appointment with Jesus. He only expected to see Jesus from a distance, but Jesus had other plans for him. He had a divine appointment with him and his life was changed forever. The Lord loves to give us divine appointments, connecting us with the right people at the right time.

When I was a young minister, I felt an impression to pray for "a man from Japan who would come to help me." I prayed week after week for this man from Japan. At this point in my life, I did not know anyone from Japan. Many years later during a leadership conference, I met some new friends and joined them for breakfast. One of my new friends' parents had come from Asia. I told him about my prayer for a man from Japan who would come to help me. He stood up at the breakfast table and said, "I am your man from Japan! God has called me to help you." I was stunned.

Over the next few years, this amazing "man from Japan" flew at his own expense to our offices in Pennsylvania to consult with our team free of charge. He has been a great blessing to us and has helped us again and again. This was the result of a divine appointment and my honoring of the supernatural impression from God about a man from Japan.

My colleague Peter Bunton told me recently, "I was at college—young, trying to get educated and travelling the world. At age twenty I moved to study in Greece and later headed to study in Munich, Germany. I knew no one in Munich and wondered if I might need some help along the way. Through an acquaintance I was given the name and address of a lady serving as a missionary in Munich. I wrote to her to make contact (this was in the days of letters, not e-mails). We planned to get in touch. Some months later I arranged to fly from Greece to Germany. Although I had an address for the missionary woman, I flew without knowing neither how I would get into the city, nor where I would stay that night."

"Through Psalm 32:8, I sensed that God would guide me. I arrived at the airport in Thessaloniki, Greece, where some friends had come to see me off. They recognized an older woman they knew and introduced us. She was booked on the same flight as me. As we chatted during the flight I mentioned the name of the one contact I had. My fellow passenger looked surprised and said, 'She will be at the airport to meet me!' My contact in Munich had not known that I was arriving in Germany that day, nor that I would be on the same flight as her friend who was sitting next to me on the plane."

"That was not a coincidence! God directed our meeting. Despite my youthful ignorance and concern for how I was going to figure out life in Germany, God arranged for the one person I had written to months before to be there to meet my fellow passenger. Without knowing it, she was there for me too! My contact and her friend provided accommodation for me and even the following day drove me to where I needed to be. God certainly did orchestrate my steps and took care of me as I was learning, as a young Christian, to follow Him."

REFLECTION
Have you ever had a divine appointment? Explain.

Expect supernatural divine appointments in your life! Listen to the still small voice of the Holy Spirit and see what God will do! Expect that you will encounter the supernatural.

God Encounters Ordinary People in Supernatural Ways

God loves to use ordinary people to fulfill His purposes. "Now when they saw the boldness of Peter and John, and perceived that they were uneducated and untrained men, they marveled. And they realized that they had been with Jesus" (Acts 4:13).

Kevin Kazemi, Merle Shenk and I, as co-authors of this book, are all ordinary guys, but we have an extraordinary

God living inside of us. And our amazing God wants each one of us who know Jesus to live in communion with Him so that we can encounter the supernatural minute by minute.

Living a supernatural lifestyle is not only for a chosen few; it is for everyone, including you. Most of us desire to be used by God, but life is filled with rushing here and there for appointments, work, children's activities and everyday responsibilities. It is often in these ordinary activities that we can encounter the Lord and experience supernatural divine appointments. That's where God wants to use us.

> Living a supernatural lifestyle is not only for a chosen few; it is for everyone, including you.

I am a common, ordinary guy who believes that God can use me to tell others about Jesus while I go about my daily life. I have missed opportunities many times, but the Lord continues to give me grace and more chances to trust that He will use me as I encounter the supernatural and touch others in supernatural ways.

Recently as I was driving through my hometown, I felt hungry for Chinese food. I turned into a local Chinese restaurant and walked inside.

The Chinese lady who was my server seemed troubled. I asked her how she was doing and the conversation turned towards spiritual things. I told her that Jesus really loved her and asked her if she knew this. She shook her head and then proceeded to tell me she had never heard anyone say this before. I was amazed. This was happening about three miles from my home in the "Bible belt" where we live. I asked if I could pray for her, and she gave a nod to indicate that it would be okay. I prayed and asked the Lord to reveal Himself to her. She thanked me sincerely.

Remember, this divine appointment that gave me an opportunity to tell someone who did not know that Jesus loved her started with a nudge to eat Chinese food! I am convinced that nudge was from the Holy Spirit, and I look forward to seeing what God will continue to do in her life.

When Jesus walked the earth, He did what He did because He was the Son of Man. He also listened to the nudges of the Holy Spirit, just like you and I do. You and I can have the same kind of ministry that Jesus had because we have the same Holy Spirit that He had. It might be hard to believe, but we can do the same works that Jesus did…and greater works! Jesus himself said in John 14:12, "Anyone who believes in me will do the same works I have done, and even greater works, because I am going to be with the Father."

I encourage you to make yourself available to the Holy Spirit. It is up to Him to decide what kind of adventures you will have, but understand this: you will have adventures of the highest kind. We are all given the privilege to be in a partnership with God Himself and He has given His Holy Spirit to us as a seal and a pledge of what is to come. In this day and hour the Lord is calling His church to arise in faith, power and obedience to fulfill its ministry and destiny. If you can hear that call, then be like Samuel and say, "Lord, here am I, your servant is listening."

The same supernatural spiritual gifts portrayed in the New Testament are available to us. Start where you are. Before you try to trust God to see someone raised from the dead, you might want to trust Him to heal a backache. Just get started. Like the disciples learned from Jesus, you too can learn from others. Surround yourself with those who are mature in the supernatural gifts of the Holy Spirit so you can also grow in them.

The last chapter of the book of Acts is still being written. It is now your turn to experience the kingdom of God being manifested on earth as you encounter the Lord and His supernatural gifts of the Holy Spirit. "God has given each of you a gift from his great variety of spiritual gifts. Use them well to serve one another" (1 Peter 4:10).

> **REFLECTION**
> *How has this book helped you to encounter the supernatural and prepare you to minister to others in the power of the Holy Spirit?*

Let's expect our God to use each of us to minister to others in the power of the Holy Spirit through supernatural encounters with the Lord that will bring glory to Him! Exciting days ahead!

Endnotes

Chapter 1

[1] Matthew Henry, retrieved from The Preacher's Word: Great Verses of the Bible (November 22, 2017) *https://thepreachersword.com/2017/11/22/great-verses-of-the-bible-1thessalonians-518*.

Chapter 2

[1] Leonard Ravenhill, *Why Revival Tarries* (Bloomington, MN, Bethany House Publishers, 1987).

[2] T.L. Osborn, *Soul Winning: A Classic on Biblical Christianity* (Tulsa, OK, Osborn Ministries International, 1963).

Chapter 3

[1] James Strong, *Strong's Exhaustive Concordance of the Bible* (Peabody, MS, Hendrickson Publishers, Inc., 2007).

Chapter 5

[1] Bill Johnson, *God is Good* (Shippensburg, PA: Destiny Image Publishers, 2016).

Chapter 6

[1] Shawn Bolz, *God Secrets: A life filled with words of knowledge* (Studio City, CA: ICreate Productions, 2017).

Chapter 7

1. John Eldredge, *Fathered by God: Learning What your Dad could Never Teach You* (Nashville, TN, Thomas Nelson Inc., 2009).

2. Dave Hess, *Hope Beyond Reason: Embraced by God's Presence in the Toughest of Times* (Shippensburg, PA, Destiny Image Publishers, 2008).

Chapter 8

1. Derek Prince, *The Gifts of the Spirit*, (Kensington, PA: Whitaker House, 2007), p. 205.

2. Larry Kreider and Dennis DeGrasse, *Supernatural Living* (Shippensburg, PA, Destiny Image Publishers, 2009).

Chapter 1 Outline
Exploring the Supernatural

1. **The supernatural world we live in**
   a. The supernatural world that surrounds us is real and highly influential in our lives.
   b. The supernatural powers of God and Satan are both in competition for the destiny of our lives.
   c. Elisha's servant could not see what was happening in the spirit realm until God opened his spiritual eyes (2 Kings 6). We can also pray that our eyes will be opened so that we will see the unseen world from God's perspective.

2. **Being born again is a supernatural experience**
   a. Each one of us has a "God story" about how we gave our lives to Christ and the difference He has made in our lives.
   b. Our decision to receive Christ releases something supernatural; it is more about what God does for us than about our own decision to follow Christ (John 6:44).
   c. True conversion is a supernatural experience. God is calling us to live by faith and experience His supernatural power.

3. **Holy Spirit baptism releases the supernatural**
   a. Being baptized in the Holy Spirit opens us to God's supernatural world. It changes how we see things and increases our faith (Acs 1:4-8).
   b. All genuine believers have the Spirit of God dwelling in them, but there is a difference between receiving the Holy Spirit at the time of spiritual rebirth and being filled with the Holy Spirit.
   c. We can be filled with the Holy Spirit again and again. The same disciples who were filled with the Holy Spirit in Acts 2 were again filled in Acts 4:31.

Teaching Outline

4. **Faith releases the supernatural**
   a. Faith releases the supernatural in our lives, and "without faith, it is impossible to please God" (Hebrews 11:6).
   b. God wants us to experience His supernatural life flowing through us as we believe.

5. **Building our faith**
   a. Reading and meditating on the Word of God builds our faith (Romans 10:17).
   b. Larry's translator in Indonesia received the supernatural ability to understand and speak English.
   c. The supernatural was normal in Jesus' ministry, but in His home town He could not do many miracles due to lack of faith (Mark 6:5-6). Faith and the supernatural go hand in hand.

6. **Supernatural provision**
   a. There are amazing stories of supernatural provision in the Bible, including manna for the children of Israel, Jesus feeding the 5,000 and money in the fish's mouth to pay taxes.
   b. An attitude of thanksgiving is a key to experiencing supernatural provision (I Thessalonians 5:18).
   c. God's provision comes in many ways; when people traveled with Jesus and provided for Him (Luke 8:1-3), that was also provision from the hand of God.

7. **Supernatural healing**
   a. The Bible says "they will lay hands on the sick, and they will recover" (Mark 16:18).
   b. God wants us to trust Him for His supernatural power to touch and change those for whom we pray.
   c. We do the praying and believing in faith—God does the healing (Psalm 103:3).

Chapter 2 Outline
Experiencing the Fear of the Lord

1. **From the East to the West**
   a. Kevin's testimony of growing up in a Muslim family and their escape to Sweden demonstrates the power of God.
   b. Jesus appeared to Kevin's mom in a vision and that supernatural encounter led to her salvation.
   c. When Kevin had a radical encounter with God, he was instantly set free from drug addiction and miraculously saved.

2. **God's heart for the nations**
   a. God loves every nation and is passionate to see every person—regardless of religion, race or culture—come to Him (John 3:16).
   b. The nations of the world are looking for the reality of Jesus.
   c. God is raising a generation that has an urgency in their hearts to represent the reality of Christ and the knowledge of His love to a lost and dying world (2 Peter 3:9).

3. **Reveal yourself to me**
   a. Each one of us needs a personal encounter with the Lord.
   b. Jesus promised that if we obey Him, He would manifest or reveal Himself to us (John 14:21).
   c. A close and intimate relationship with Jesus Christ will cause us to be His witnesses to a lost and dying world.

4. **The true supernatural power of Jesus**
   a. God's supernatural power working through a generation that knows His reality is the only thing that can change this world.
   b. Out of obedience, Kevin started a Bible study in Sweden and it grew very quickly (Mark 16:20).

Teaching Outline

    c. One woman in the Bible study group had visions of Jesus coming and standing next to her bed. Although she found this frightening, it caused her to get right with God.

5. **Seen by multitudes**
    a. Jesus appeared to His disciples for forty days after His resurrection. Ordinary people just like us walked, talked and ate with the Lord Jesus in His resurrected body (Acts 1:3).
    b. When men and women were used by God in a mighty supernatural way in the Bible, it was not because of their own greatness, but God's. Apart from the blood of Christ, we have nothing (James 5:17-18).
    c. Our theological boundaries are some of the greatest hindrances that keep us from a life-changing encounter with the Lord. Every encounter in Scripture is an invitation to step out of those limitations and into His supernatural world.

6. **Unusual expectation**
    a. Kevin's encounter with the presence of God caused him to be filled with the fear of the Lord, yet also brought deep peace.
    b. The Israelites chose to stay at a distance because of the dread of God's presence rather than, like Moses, approach the thick darkness where God dwelled. (Exodus 20:19-21).
    c. We need to experience a purification before we can receive a revelation of God's glory.

7. **The covering of His hand**
    a. Kevin experienced a visitation from the Lord that was a call to holiness and separation unto God (Acts 2:2).
    b. Our Father God desires to manifest Himself to us (Exodus 33:11, 22).
    c. A revelation of the love of God will cause us to see the beauty of repentance and will birth a passion for purity within.

Chapter 3 Outline
A Visitation from God

1. **The Spirit of the fear of the Lord**
   a. We need the fear of the Lord in our lives if we desire to experience more of His glory.
   b. A great level of holiness was required in the foundation of the New Testament church. If we want to see that same power, we also need to sanctify our hearts and set ourselves apart for God (Acts 5:3-11).
   c. Whenever we see a greater manifestation of the glory of the Lord, we also see a greater dimension of the fear of the Lord coming upon God's people (I Peter 3:15).

2. **Delighting in the fear of the Lord**
   a. Many times we have a wrong picture about our heavenly Father's heart because of painful experiences in life.
   b. One of the primary reasons for Jesus coming to earth was to reveal the Father heart of God and restore the relationship that was lost in the garden when mankind fell into sin.
   c. True repentance causes us to delight in walking in the fear of the Lord (Psalm 128:1).

3. **The path to knowing God's goodness**
   a. The Bible says that God spoke with Moses face to face (Numbers 12:8).
   b. Moses experienced the power of God in amazing ways, yet he cried out for more of God (Exodus 33:11-13).
   c. The fear of the Lord at work in our hearts will bring us into a greater dimension of God's glory.

Teaching Outline

4. **He has heard your cry**
   a. We can only reveal Jesus to the world when He has become real to us first.
   b. The desire of our Lord to reveal Himself to us is greater than our desire to be used by Him (Jeremiah 29:14).
   c. Allowing the purifying fire of God to burn away any dross in our hearts will lead to a life filled with supernatural encounters (Matthew 5:8).

5. **The time of visitation**
   a. Kevin testifies of the Lord appearing to him with a holy presence.
   b. God rejoices over His people (Zephaniah 3:17).
   c. There are times when the Word of God and presence of God manifest in the natural realm (Matthew 17:6).

6. **Invisible becoming visible**
   a. The apostles of the New Testament, including Paul, all had a personal encounter with the risen Lord (I John 1:1).
   b. From the book of Genesis to the book of Revelation, God appeared in many different ways to His people (Hebrews 1:1).
   c. The Word of God is the final authority over our lives and our experiences. We should never try to dictate what God can or cannot say to us based on our own personal theology or experiences.

7. **The power of God**
   a. God desires to be personally involved in our lives (I Corinthians 2:1-5).
   b. It is our responsibility to seek the Lord with our whole heart.
   c. An encounter with the Lord gives a passion to share the love of God and power of God with others.

Chapter 4 Outline
Being Changed by His Presence

1. **A Demonstration of God's Power**
   a. During a healing meeting, Kevin invited those who needed healing to touch the hem of Jesus garment.
   b. God desires to demonstrate His power through us.
   c. The church of the living God is called to bring people into an encounter with His presence, but not to gather people to hear our own human wisdom.

2. **God's presence brings healing**
   a. A word of knowledge led to healing for a woman with cancer through a supernatural, tangible flow of God's power through Kevin.
   b. Jesus Christ is still doing miracles today. There is power in the name of Jesus.

3. **The kingdom of God is within us**
   a. The spiritual kingdom is present among His people through the indwelling of the Holy Spirit.
   b. We can experience the fullness of Jesus Christ; the kingdom of God is within us as God brings heaven to earth (Luke 17:20-21).
   c. God wants to touch the world, but can only do it through His body, the church. We are the church of the living God.

4. **Good stewardship is everything**
   a. Paul was entrusted with a mystery regarding Christ in us. This speaks of the presence of God in our lives.
   b. We need to be continually conscious of the presence of the Lord in order to be good stewards of His presence.

c. God does not only want to visit us occasionally and manifest His presence now and then, He wants to live permanently within us (John 1:32).

5. His presence will change you
   a. Kevin had the opportunity to share his faith in Jesus with a young man from Iran. It was a shock to this young man to learn that Kevin was a follower of Jesus even though he was born in Iran.
   b. The one who answers prayers and delivers us from the power of the enemy is Jesus Christ, the Son of the living God.

6. What shall I do to be saved?
   a. An Iranian young man had an encounter with the Lord and asked "What shall I do to be saved?" Thereafter, he wanted a Bible in the Farsi language, and God arranged that he would get one.
   b. Many times God wants to set up a divine appointment between us and someone who needs to hear of His love.

7. The reality of Jesus
   a. A young man of the Muslim faith had a dream in which he saw Muhammad, Buddha and other spiritual leaders bowing down to Jesus.
   b. The world is looking for the reality of Jesus. The only way we can make Him real to others is for Him to first become real to us (Acts 3:6).

Chapter 5 Outline
Experiencing His Presence

1. **Walking with God**
   a. Jesus' purpose in coming to earth was to restore us into relationship with God and send us out to minister to others (Mark 3:14-15).
   b. Jesus modeled many things while he was on earth: how to relate to those who do not know Christ, how to live a life without sin, how to experience the love of the Father, and how to work with the Holy Spirit.
   c. The enemy speaks discouragement to us while the Father gives words of life. We need to discern the difference and be careful not to listen to or believe the voice of the enemy.

2. **Receiving through time with God**
   a. Our personal times with God empower us to minister life to others (Matthew 10:7-8).
   b. In the secret place of communion with God, we receive the power and grace for daily living (Romans 8:2).
   c. The inner life with God, which is for everybody, is governed by the law of love that constrains us from doing anything that violates God's love for us or ours for Him (Psalm 119:11).

3. **Moving with the Holy Spirit**
   a. The Holy Spirit helps us steward our inner life with God; He leads us into truth and makes known to us what we need to know (John 14:16-17).
   b. One of the ways the Holy Spirit gives words of knowledge (Merle's experience), is through timely Scripture references that provide applicable guidance in different situations.
   c. The Holy Spirit appropriates all that God has for us in our relationship with Him and keeps us connected to the Father.

Teaching Outline

4. **God with you: Emmanuel**
   a. Core beliefs, determined by our experiences, can influence the ways in which we view the world, ourselves and others.
   b. Signs and wonders are never a substitute for God's presence. His presence and the knowledge of His love are the most supernatural things we can ever experience.
   c. God's presence gives us courage and takes away fear (Joshua 1:9).

5. **Knowing the heavenly Father**
   a. Revealing the Father to us was one of Jesus' main purposes for coming to earth (Matthew 5:45-48).
   b. God's love is not a reward for our performance; we never have to fear not being loved.
   c. An understanding of God's unconditional love empowers us to minister to others. Jesus says that we are to love others in the same way that God loves them (Luke 15).

6. **What makes a person valuable?**
   a. A coin or currency note has value because of the image that is stamped on it. Every person is valuable because every person is created in the image and likeness of God.
   b. God loved us before we ever loved Him. He loves and values each of us before we welcome Him into our lives.
   c. An open-hearted embrace toward others is one of the keys to seeing the supernatural work of God flow through us.

7. **Helping people become followers**
   a. One way we can understand the definition of a follower of Jesus is to know someone who is literally following Him.
   b. The goal in ministering supernaturally is to inspire others to follow Jesus more closely (Acts 17:26-27).

Chapter 6 Outline
Ministering with Jesus

1. **The kingdom of God is available to us**
   a. The kingdom of God is here with us now close enough for us to touch. It is appropriated to us by the Holy Spirit (Luke 17:20-21).
   b. We tend to subconsciously believe that we only truly deserve what we can earn. But God makes so much more available to us than what we deserve (Matthew 10:8).
   c. There could be differences in the way different cultures approach their walk with God and experience their faith.

2. **What are we assuming?**
   a. It is very possible for us to miss the things that God is doing in our midst just as the Pharisees who had dedicated their lives to the study of Scripture missed the reality of Jesus as Messiah.
   b. Our assumptions about how God will move can distort the work of the Holy Spirit flowing through us to others.
   c. Merle's testimony about misunderstanding a vision that he had for a young man is an example showing that at times we can fail to see what God is doing.

3. **Carrying Jesus to others**
   a. God is already working in the places that we are going to minister. In order to minister effectively we need to find out what God is doing and how to join Him in it (John 15:17).
   b. It is very powerful when people hear God through His Word for themselves.
   c. The Bible Study method that Merle describes facilitates the process of people hearing from the Lord personally.

Teaching Outline

4. **Learning to listen**
   a. Gifts of the Holy Spirit known as revelatory gifts are the gifts of prophecy, words of wisdom and words of knowledge.
   b. Through the supernatural gifts of the Spirit we might sense many needs in people around us, but we are only responsible to minister as God directs.
   c. Understanding that we are only a mouthpiece of God and asking Him for direction takes off the pressure to perform.

5. **The Holy Spirit presents God's love**
   a. God communicates His love and concern for His children through the gifts of Holy Spirit (John 10:27).
   b. Merle's testimony about a word of knowledge regarding the name Jaclyn and the experience of being an orphan illustrates how much God cares for each one.

6. **Words of knowledge for healing**
   a. The Holy Spirit could give a thought or picture about a certain part of the human body when He wants to heal.
   b. We might not understand why some people get healed and others do not, but we still need to obediently pray for healing.
   c. When we receive words of knowledge during ministry, we are encouraged to ask people if a specific need is present and then pray, asking God to heal.

7. **Knowing the mind of Christ**
   a. The human brain is biologically equipped to develop through social interactions. The more we spend time with Christ, the more we become like Him and reflect His values.
   b. God often communicates with us through dreams or visions that we receive through the screen of the imagination.
   c. When our minds are burdened with fear or shame, it becomes more difficult to receive God's thoughts.

Chapter 7 Outline
Growing in a Supernatural Lifestyle

1. **Visions of Angels**
   a. Miracles do not happen by following formulas or prescribed prayers. Each situation is different and the Holy spirit works in different ways.
   b. A lady was healed from HIV/Aids after Merle and those with him prayed according to visions of angels (Hebrews 1:4).

2. **Fathered by God through a stranger**
   a. Merle's testimony about finding someone to help him in a time of need while in line in a bank illustrates how God uses others supernaturally.
   b. If we are open to the work of the Holy Spirit in our lives, He will use us to minister and speak His wisdom to others (John 6:45).
   c. God holds all the knowledge that we need for challenging situations in our lives. There is always a solution in His mind (John 14:3).

3. **God's touch through others**
   a. Ministering the love of the Father to others could involve hugs and physical touch (John 1:18).
   b. Many people are deeply hungry for God's love.
   c. The love of the Father is available to us today, in our present place and situation (John 14:3).

4. **The joy of healing**
   a. Merle gives the testimony of the healing of a young girl who was hospitalized. Her mother was a recent convert from Islam to Christ.

b. When we have reached the end of what we know, we need to stand firm in faith and believe that God's promises will be fulfilled (Ephesians 6:13-14).

5. Encounters that bring healing
   a. When we are available to pray for others with authority, God moves through us to touch and heal (Acts 14:9-10).
   b. Every encounter that we have with other people should be an opportunity for God to move.
   c. We can create an atmosphere of God's presence around us in our lives and homes through our relationship with Him.

6. Miracles of provision
   a. Merle shares several testimonies about how God provided for them miraculously (Philippians 4:19).
   b. Generous giving, even laying down possessions that we treasure, demonstrates our surrender to the Lord and our total trust (2 Corinthians 9:7-8).
   c. Trusting God is not always easy, but it is worth it.

7. Catalyst relationships
   a. Working together with empowering relationships can help push us beyond the normal comfort level in our lives (Hebrews 10:24).
   b. Jesus sent disciples out in groups of two for a reason (Acts 16:25).
   c. It is important to value relationships with those who stir up our faith, and also to avoid relationships that drain our faith.

Chapter 8 Outline
You Too can Encounter the Supernatural

1. **Angelic protection**
    a. Angels, according to the Scriptures, provide supernatural protection to those who are following Christ (Hebrews 1:14).
    b. We may not always be aware of the presence of angels around us, but God has sent angels to protect His children.
    c. We can pray that our eyes will be opened to see and understand God's supernatural protection (Hebrews 13:2).

2. **Weapons of warfare**
    a. The Lord gives us three powerful spiritual weapons to defeat the spirits of darkness: the name of Jesus Christ, the blood of Jesus, and the word of our testimony (Revelation 12:11).
    b. Demons are afraid of the name and blood of Jesus (James 4:7-8).
    c. Our testimony is a confession of what the Lord has done in our lives and what God is saying about us.

3. **A supernatural gift of faith**
    a. The gift of faith is the special ability that God gives us to believe, with extraordinary confidence and unwavering faith, that He will fulfill His promises (Mark 11:24).
    b. A person with the gift of faith acts in complete confidence in God's ability to overcome obstacles and to provide.
    c. The gift of wisdom gives us the supernatural ability to properly use the knowledge we receive from God.

4. **Testing supernatural manifestations**
    a. Supernatural prophecies and gifts need to be tested by the Scriptures (I Thessalonians 5:19-21).

    b. We must test a prophetic word for its meaning (application) and timing.
    c. Not many people will begin by prophesying perfectly. Operating in any spiritual gift takes practice (Romans 12:6).

5. Praying in tongues bypasses the devil
    a. According to Scriptures, we can pray in two ways: with our mind and with our spirit. Both are under the influence of the Holy Spirit (I Corinthians 14:14-15).
    b. When we pray with our spirit, we do not understand what we are saying but our heavenly Father does.
    c. The most important use of the gift of tongues is for our own personal devotional life. When we pray in tongues, we are building ourselves up in the holy faith (Jude 1:20).

6. Supernatural divine appointments
    a. Zacchaeus had a divine appointment with Jesus, and his life was changed forever (Luke 19:1-10).
    b. The Lord loves to give us divine appointments, connecting us with the right people at the right time (Psalm 32:8).
    c. Expect supernatural divine appointments; expect that you will encounter the supernatural.

7. God encounters ordinary people in supernatural ways
    a. God loves to use ordinary people to fulfill His purposes. Living a supernatural lifestyle is not only for a chosen few; it is for everyone (Acts 4:13).
    b. As believers in Christ, we are called to have the same type of ministry that Jesus had because the same Holy Spirit is available to us.
    c. We are encouraged to expect God to use us to minister to others in the power of the Holy Spirit that will bring glory to Him (I Peter 4:10).

Reflection journaling space

Chapter 1 **Exploring the Supernatural**

Day 1 *Describe the differences between the supernatural world and the natural world. Which is more important? Why?*

Is what we perceive always accurate? Why or why not?

Day 2 *Explain the differences between following Christ and living a supernatural life.*

How are you experiencing the supernatural life of Christ in your life today?

Day 3 *How do you know that you have been baptized in the Holy Spirit?*

How does being baptized in the Holy Spirit open us to the supernatural power of Jesus Christ?

Day 4 *Why is faith important in order to experience the supernatural?*

Give an example of a time you experienced the supernatural power of God in your life.

Day 5 Name ways that we can practically build our faith.

What are some scriptural examples of living in the supernatural that you would love to experience?

Day 6 Give examples of supernatural provision from the Scriptures. Give examples of supernatural provision that you have experienced.

Explain the importance of living with an attitude of thanksgiving.

Day 7 How can we experience supernatural healing through our lives?

What can we learn from the story of the man in prison who received a supernatural healing?

Reflection journaling space

Chapter 2 **Experiencing the Fear of the Lord**

Day 1 *Explain how you have experienced God's love as an individual.*

Write your testimony and condense it until you can say it within a two-minute time frame.

Day 2 *Explain how you can discover God's heart for the nations. Give a personal example.*

What are some of the ways the Lord reveals Himself to Muslims?

Day 3 *Does asking for more of God display a lack of faith? In what ways are you pursuing the supernatural?*

According to T. L. Osborn's testimony, what event became the turning point of his life and ministry?

Day 4 *Are there any areas of life in which God is calling you to a deeper level of obedience? If so, what are they?*

In what ways has God revealed Himself to you?

Day 5 *Why do you think the Lord appeared to people in the Bible? Why did He appear to so many?*

In what ways have you experienced God's resurrection power in and through your life?

Day 6 *Do you expect to experience the supernatural in your life? Is it important to you?*

How is God inviting you into a deeper experience of Himself?

Day 7 *Do you believe that Jesus desires to reveal Himself to you and give you a deeper experience of Himself?*

Have you invited the fire of the Lord to purge you from compromise? If yes, is your life yielded to His purging fire?

Reflection journaling space

Chapter 3 **The Spirit of the Fear of the Lord**

Day 1 *Describe the difference between walking in the fear of the Lord and the lack of the fear of the Lord in our lives.*

Are there ways you or your ministry can handle God's presence with respect and honor? Why is it important to do so?

Day 2 *Explain in your own words how you think Jesus finds His delight in the fear of God.*

What is the difference between being afraid of God or walking in the fear of God?

Day 3 *What are some of the ways we can come to know the nature and character of God?*

Why is it essential to experience the goodness of God in our lives?

Day 4 *What are some things in your life that keep you from the supernatural?*

What does it mean to search for God with all of our heart? Give some personal examples.

Day 5 *Give biblical examples of when heaven came down to earth in supernatural ways. How can heaven become real in our lives and churches?*

How is the Lord rejoicing over you in this season of your life?

Day 6 *Explain the kind of relationship Abraham had with God.*

Have you ever had the invisible becoming visible in your life? Explain.

Day 7 *How is the wisdom of man different from the revelation and power of God?*

In what ways has Jesus Christ revealed Himself to you?

Reflection journaling space

Chapter 4 **The Power of Forgiveness**

Day 1 *What is the main reason for the spirit of wisdom and revelation according to Ephesians 1:17?*

What is the difference between the power of God and the wisdom of words?

Day 2 *When have you experienced the power of God to heal?*

How do the presence of God and the power of God correspond?

Day 3 *What did the Lord Jesus say when asked about the coming of the kingdom in Luke 17:20-21?*

Though we believe in the coming kingdom, why is it important to experience the Kingdom of God now?

Day 4 *Is hospitality important to you or in your culture? Give some examples of how it is practiced.*

In what ways do you experience God's presence in your life or ministry? How can you be a better steward of His presence?

Day 5 *How does being continually conscious of God change us?*

In what ways have you allowed God's love to touch those around you?

Day 6 *What do you remember about your salvation experience? Or, if you are not born again, what do you feel you need to do to respond to God's love for you?*

What are some of the ways God reaches out to Muslims in order to reveal His love and power?

Day 7 *Do you expect God to manifest himself through you? If yes, how? If not, why not?*

Explain why you can't give what you don't have.

Reflection journaling space

Chapter 5 **Ministering with Jesus**

Day 1 *What thoughts come to mind regarding what you believe about yourself and/or what you believe about God and His thoughts toward you?*

Do the things you believe deep in your core agree with the voice of God, or with the voice of the enemy? Explain.

Day 2 *What can you do today to cultivate your inner walk with the Lord? Why is it so important?*

Is there anything that you need to stop doing or not allow in your life because it is causing your inner life with God to deteriorate?

Day 3 *Have you invited the Holy Spirit to fill you continually?*

Why is it to our advantage to have the Holy Spirit continually connecting us to God?

Day 4 *Why do you think assurance of God's presence is important in living a supernatural life?*

What are ways in which you know that God is with you?

Day 5 *Why is it important to receive a deep and enduring revelation of God's love for us?*

How is it possible to love like God loves?

Day 6 *Do you treat others according to their created value? What does the way you treat others say about you?*

Name a person about whom you should adjust your mindset in order to be in line with God's perspective.

Day 7 *Where are you standing in relationship to God according to the example demonstrated? Are you facing towards Jesus, away from Him, or somewhere in between?*

What can you do today to help others turn toward or step toward God?

Reflection journaling space

Chapter 6 **Ministering to Jesus**

Day 1 *Has your culture taught you to receive what you deserve or receive whatever is available?*

How can you share what is available in God's Kingdom with others around you?

Day 2 *How can our assumptions cause us to miss what God is doing around us?*

If we receive prophetic insights, words or impressions for others, how can we make sure that we do not mix in our own assumptions when sharing them?

Day 3 *How do you know when God is working on drawing someone to Himself in your life?*

What are ways that you can help others find Jesus?

Day 4 *Why is it important to seek God's direction about ministering to needs in other's lives?*

Do you ever feel responsible for every problem that you see?

Day 5 *In what ways have you seen God's love communicated through the gifts of the Holy Spirit?*

Have you ever considered that the purpose of gifts of the Holy Spirit flowing through you is so that God can love others through you?

Day 6 *Have you ever specifically prayed out loud for a person to be healed?*

What can you do to see healings take place on a regular basis?

Day 7 *We often talk about fasting from food. In what ways can you fast from negativity in order to free your mind from the constant burden of troubling thoughts?*

Are there any impure thoughts, idols, or deceit you need to repent of so your heart and mind are free to engage with God's thoughts?

Reflection journaling space

Chapter 7 **Growing in a Supernatural Lifestyle**

Day 1 *Do you feel ready for God to use you in unexpected ways? Are you ready for Him to use the screen of your imagination?*

When it is time to pray for challenging scenarios, what things can you do to help you focus on the truth of God and not be overwhelmed by the problem?

Day 2 *How has God used others to "father" you in your life?*

What types of things can hinder us from experiencing divine encounters?

Day 3 *Why is it important for us to receive the affection of God's heart?*

What other Scriptures can you think of that speak of Jesus bringing us into God's love?

Day 4 *What are promises of God that you are standing for?*

What are ways that you have seen God do mighty things because of someone standing firm in faith?

Day 5 *What can you do to create an atmosphere of expectation of miracles in your home?*

What are some challenges that you face when you are with others and you want to suggest praying together?

Day 6 *In what ways have you experienced unexpected provision in your life?*

If God would ask you to lay your dearest treasures out before the Lord as an act of offering and worship, would you be willing to do so?

Day 7 *Why do you think Jesus sent people out in teams of two or more to minister?*

Are there people in your life who function as a catalyst to helping you experience more of God? What can you do to intentionally value these relationships?

Reflection journaling space

Chapter 8 **You Too can Encounter the Supernatural**

Day 1 *Have you ever experienced angelic protection? What was it like? How do we know we have angels protecting us?*

Have you ever sensed the presence of evil spirits? What did it feel like?

Day 2 *What are the three weapons the Lord gives to us so we can defeat the spirits of darkness?*

Give an example from your life when you have used any of these spiritual weapons. If you have not used any, how are you planning to use them in the future?

Day 3 *Have you ever experienced a gift of faith? Explain.*

Have you ever experienced a gift of knowledge or a gift of wisdom? Explain.

Day 4 *Have you ever received a prophecy that was life-changing for you? Explain.*

Have you ever received a prophecy, but when you tested it biblically, you realized it was not a word you should apply to your life? Explain.

Day 5 *What are some of the different types of tongues we read about in the Bible?*

Have you ever spoken in tongues? If you have not but you want to, find someone who has received this gift and ask them to pray for you.

Day 6 *Explain how Zacchaeus' life was changed through a divine appointment with Jesus.*

Have you ever had a divine appointment? Explain.

Day 7 *How did Jesus do supernatural works? How can we do the same?*

How has this book helped you to encounter the supernatural and prepare you to minister to others in the power of the Holy Spirit?

Steps to being filled with the Holy Spirit

1. **Realize that every believer has the Holy Spirit** living in him or her (Rom. 8:9, 1 Cor. 3:16).
2. **Recognize the difference** between having the Holy Spirit living in us and being filled with the Holy Spirit (John 20:22, Acts 2:1-4).
3. **Being filled with the Holy Spirit gives us spiritual power** (Acts 1:8). The most common evidence of being filled with the Holy Spirit is prophesying—proclaiming the truth, and speaking in tongues—speaking in a heavenly language (Acts chapters 2, 4, 8, 9, 10, 19 and 1 Cor. 14:14-15).
4. **God gives the Holy Spirit to those who ask Him** (Gal. 3:14; Luke 11:11-13).
5. **People in the Bible often received the Holy Spirit through the laying on of hands** (Acts 9:17 and Acts 19:1-7).
6. **When we receive the Holy Spirit, we receive this gift** with the understanding that nine spiritual gifts are contained within this one gift, and God will teach us how to use each of these individual gifts (1 Cor. 12:7-10).
7. **We need to be filled with the Holy Spirit again and again** because we leak! (Acts 4:31, Eph. 5:18).

Taken from *How Can I Be Filled with the Holy Spirit?* by Larry Kreider, 32 pages: $1.99 Visit www.h2hp.com

Larry Kreider

Larry Kreider serves as International Director of DOVE International, a network of churches throughout the world. For more than three decades, DOVE has used the New Testament "house to house" strategy of building the church with small groups.

As founder of DOVE International, Larry initially served for fifteen years as senior pastor of DOVE Christian Fellowship in Pennsylvania, which grew from a single small group to more than 2,300 believers in ten years. Today, DOVE believers meet in more than 500 congregations and in thousands of small groups in five continents of the world.

In 1971, Larry and his wife, LaVerne, helped establish a youth ministry that targeted unchurched youth in northern Lancaster County, Pennsylvania. DOVE grew out of the ensuing need for a flexible New Testament-style church that could assist these new believers.

Larry and LaVerne teach worldwide and encourage believers to reach out from house to house, city to city and nation to nation, and empower and train others to do the same.

Larry writes for Christian periodicals and has written more than forty books that have sold over 500,000 copies, with many translated into other languages. Larry earned his Masters of Ministry with a concentration on leadership from Southwestern Christian University. He and his wife have been married forty-six years and live in Lititz, Pennsylvania. They enjoy spending time with their four amazing children, two sons-in-law, a daughter-in-law and six amazing grandkids.

Read Larry's blog at www.dcfi.org/blog
Like Larry and LaVerne Kreider on Facebook
Follow Larry Kreider on Twitter

Kevin Kasemi

Kevin's journey from an abused and disaffected teen to a man who treks the globe in God's service is a great miracle of God! Kevin was born in Iran to a Muslim family, raised in Sweden and radically delivered out of a lifestyle of drugs and crime in 2004 when he converted to Christianity at a conference in Armenia. His story carries a supernatural anointing that has brought great refreshing and salvation to many around the world.

Kevin met his wife Mariella from the Netherlands in a YWAM discipleship training school in 2006 and they married in 2008. They served as missionaries for many years in Cape Town, South Africa.

As a prophetic healing evangelist, Kevin and Mariella are the founders of Flames Of Passion Ministries. Having travelled to over forty-five nations, they sense a call of God to minister around the world and see people being touched, healed and delivered by the tangible anointing of the Holy Spirit. They also have a strong passion to see the lost turn to Jesus Christ and see the intimate fellowship with the person of the Holy Spirit being restored to this generation. They believe in a big God and have a global vision to see His Kingdom advance.

For more information, visit www.flamesofpassion.org

Merle Shenk

Merle Shenk and his wife Cheree serve in the ministry of the DOVE International family. Merle is an associate pastor at Newport Church in Elm, PA, and serves as resource director for church planting for DOVE USA. Together they lead the apostolic teams for DOVE South Africa and DOVE Zambia.

In 2004 the Shenks moved to South Africa, where they were involved in planting a multi-ethnic church in Cape Town. Merle initiated Bible School training courses, as well as a correspondence Bible School. He also pioneered a school of supernatural ministry, and traveled as an itinerant minister wherever God sent him. The seasons of sowing into evangelism, supernatural ministry and leadership continue to be threads of God in their ministry to others.

In 2014, Merle received a clear word of the Lord sending them back to the USA. Knowing that this was an assignment from God, they transitioned their church to faithful local leaders and relocated to the USA in 2016. Merle served as the pioneering director of HarvestNet School of Supernatural Ministry during their first year back in the States. They wrote a chapter in DOVE International's church planting book, *The Invitation*.

Merle and Cheree are parents to five children and live in Lititz, Pennsylvania. Their desire is to see everyone walk in the presence and power of Jesus.

Other books in this series

When God Seems Silent
Discovering His purposes in times of confusion and darkness
Why does it sometimes feel like God is silent? Is He hiding from us? Larry and LaVerne Kreider help us examine these questions and many of the barriers that can block the voice of God in our lives. They also reveal their own struggle with God's silences and the tremendous breakthroughs that can be discovered. *By Larry and LaVerne Kreider, 208 pages:* **$12.99**

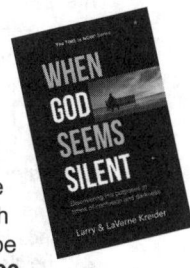

Straight Talk to Leaders
What we wish we had known when we started
Four Christian leaders disclose key leadership lessons they have learned through forty years of pastoring and establishing worldwide ministries. This illuminating book explores topics such as team building, boundaries, transitions, stress management, learning from criticism, making tough decisions and much more! *By Larry Kreider, Sam Smucker, Barry Wissler and Lester Zimmerman, 204 pages:* **$12.99**

Battle Cry for Your Marriage
Discovering breakthroughs for today's challenges
With raw honesty four couples tackle issues of spiritual, emotional and sexual intimacy along with other marital stresses. Biblically-based insights will inspire spouses to face issues, communicate honestly, find life-changing strategies and—most of all—love the One who gave them the gift of each other. *By Larry and LaVerne Kreider, Steve and Mary Prokopchak Duane and Reyna Britton, Wallace and Linda Mitchell, 204 pages:* **$12.99**

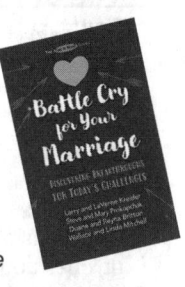

Finding Freedom
Becoming whole and living free
The struggle is real. We desire to follow Christ, but too often we find ourselves entangled and tripped up, falling back into the old patterns of our former selves. Authors examine God's Word for the answers and share from their own lives and others who have experienced God's true freedom. *By Larry Kreider, Craig and Tracie Nanna 198 pages:* **$12.99**

www.h2hp.com
Call 800.848.5892

Biblical Foundation Series
This series by Larry Kreider covers basic Christian doctrine. Practical illustrations accompany the easy-to-understand format. Use for small group teachings (48 outlines) in mentoring relationship or as a daily devotional. *By Larry Kreider, Each book has 64 pages:* **$4.99** each
12 Book Set: **$39**
Available in Spanish and French.

Titles in this series:
1. **Knowing Jesus Christ as Lord**
2. **The New Way of Living**
3. **New Testament Baptisms**
4. **Building For Eternity**
5. **Living in the Grace of God**
6. **Freedom from the Curse**
7. **Learning to Fellowship with God**
8. **What is the Church?**
9. **Authority and Accountability**
10. **God's Perspective on Finances**
11. **Called to Minister**
12. **The Great Commission**

The Cry for Spiritual Mothers and Fathers
Returning to the biblical truth of spiritual parenting is necessary so believers are not left fatherless and disconnected. Learn how loving, seasoned spiritual fathers and mothers help spiritual children reach their full potential in Christ. *By Larry Kreider, 224 pages*: **$14.99**

Your Personal House of Prayer
Christians often struggle with their prayer lives. With the unique "house plan" developed in this book, each room corresponding to a part of the Lord's Prayer, your prayer life is destined to go from duty to joy! Includes a helpful Daily Prayer Guide. *By Larry Kreider, 192 pages:* **$12.99**

Passing the 21 Tests of Leadership
Whether you are called to lead in business, your community or church, life is filled with tests! Will you be able to pass them? *By Larry Kreider, 218 pages:* **$16.99**

www.h2hp.com
Call 800.848.5892